D0176568

Two-Up

Navigating a Relationship
1,000 Miles at a Time

by

Lynda Lahman

Copyright © 2012 Lynda Lahman
All rights reserved.

ISBN: 1469913739
ISBN 13: 9781469913735

To Terry, for making dreams come true.

Acknowledgements

My friends not only put up with me while I was writing this book but also listened to my endless stories about falling in love with both Terry and motorcycling. I believe you all know who you are and how important you are to me. Your support through the years has been amazing and I am grateful.

Steve Chalmers, thank you for being such a fun introduction to this craziness. Special recognition to Mike Kneebone, Lisa Landry, Dale Wilson, Ira Agins, Tom Austin, and all of the Iron Butt Association staff and volunteers, who have created an organization and a rally second to none and in the process of welcoming me into your world became my friends. To all my motorcycling friends, thank you for understanding this insanity and always treating me as an equal, not "just a pillion."

To my FAP and ACT friends, thank you for creating a safe place for me to listen to my heart and encouraging me to take risks.

Bill Shaw, thank you for trusting me enough to make me a regular columnist in the *Iron Butt Magazine*. You gave me the courage to believe I could write something people might want to read.

Rachel Dillon, Sue Dowling, John Parrish, Kurt and Jackie Swanson, Lisa Landry and Bill Shaw, my readers, who took a risk offering me candid observations and commentary. You each pushed me to dig deeper and tell the story more fully. My book is much richer thanks to each of you.

Jerry Smith, meeting you at Gerlachfest was serendipitous. You have been an amazing editor, steering me in the right direction, challenging me to be better, and making my mistakes go away.

Steve Hobart, I can now say thank you for making us go out at o'dark thirty for the magazine cover shoot. Without planning to, you created the incredible cover for this book. Tobie Stevens, thanks for your help with photo editing, and for the picture near Big Pump.

Katie, Chris, Aaron and Jessica, thank you for finding a way to make us a family, and to your partners for joining us on this journey and letting me be a part of your lives.

And to Terry, without whom there would be no story. Your willingness to sit on the curb and figure it out means more to me than anything. Thank you for being OK with letting go of your suggested title "Riding With Terry," and most importantly, thank you for driving.

Prologue

If anyone had asked me what I thought I might be doing with my life following a divorce at age forty-nine, it never would have occurred to me to answer, "Entering a competition that involves spending eleven days riding on the back of a motorcycle around the country in a giant scavenger hunt." I thought it was enough that I was willing to risk dating and falling in love.

When I met Terry, and my friends learned he loved motorcycles, they rushed in to tell me about the dangers of riding. Having already been in the dating world, a bike seemed much safer. Terry's passion was long-distance motorcycling, and he invited me to tag along. I never imagined over the next three years I'd be entering a world that contained something called the Iron Butt Association, much less the Iron Butt Rally, an eleven-day, 11,000-mile scavenger hunt across North America. I certainly never dreamed one day we'd be entered to ride in "The World's Toughest Motorcycle Competition."

CHAPTER ONE

Match

The music drifted over the crowd as I sat on the lawn of our local winery surrounded by others of my generation singing and waving lighters in the night sky. I vaguely remembered the song from my youth but as I listened to The Moody Blues playing it live I felt tears coming to my eyes. "I Know You're Out There Somewhere" speaks of the longing for the person with whom you were meant to be. The words not only now had meaning for me, but as I looked at Terry he was crying as well as he whispered to me, "I always knew this was true, I always dreamed I'd find you."

I've never been a misty-eyed believer in fairy tales. My template for marriage was a broken one. Unlike most kids who move around a lot because one of their parents was in the military or their job required frequent relocations, I moved because my parents couldn't get their own lives together. Between them they had seven marriages and divorces, and my mom traipsed across the country dragging my brother and me with her. Growing up I often begged my mother to send me to a boarding school where I imagined a life filled with routine, where nothing ever changed. She never took me seriously.

The most stable relationship I witnessed was between my grandfather and my step-grandmother, Amy. They married before I was born and remained together, blissfully happy, for forty-four years until he died in 1996. Everyone who met them described them as the most loving, caring couple they knew. I envied their devotion to each other and the adventures they took, traveling all around the world, building friendships with everyone they met along the way. I grew up thinking relationships like theirs were rare, found mostly in romance novels. I never imagined such a life, or such a marriage, for myself.

I met my first husband, Pete, when I was twenty-three. I was just starting graduate school in Marriage and Family Therapy and eager to find a boyfriend. I had no idea what to look for in a relationship other than we should like each other and get along. I had some doubts in the very beginning, thinking we were a bit too different, and that we had come from different backgrounds. But Pete thought we belonged together, and a month later, when my landlord no longer allowed pets and my dog Jack and I needed a place to live, we moved in together. The next logical step was marriage, and over the next seven years we completed the family picture with the birth of our daughter Katie and our son Chris. Wanting a better environment than Los Angeles for raising our children, we moved to Seattle where Pete landed a job in the outdoor industry and I built a successful part-time private practice. We settled into a relatively routine suburban life, and I convinced myself I was happy enough. Stability for my kids mattered more than passion or adventure, something being a single parent of two young children wouldn't provide.

Over time, however, Pete and I admitted we were too disconnected, too different in what we wanted and in how we moved in the world. I longed for intimacy, togetherness, and sharing, while Pete desired intensity, independence, and freedom. We had tried for twenty-six years to make things work, and succeeded in many areas. We did projects well together, respected each other and cared for each other. But we weren't in love, and maybe never had been. We were good friends, good roommates, and good planners. We reached a measure of financial stability, and our kids were almost grown. We finally acknowledged it wasn't enough, and reluctantly made the decision to divorce. In the summer of 2002, just shy of forty-nine, I found myself alone with a daughter about to leave for college on the east coast, and a son starting his sophomore year of high school.

Embarking on a new life as a single woman, I moved with the kids into a condo. I had no intention of dating. Bumping into a casual friend at church one evening quickly changed my mind, and I was surprised when I fell hard for Mark and we started a relationship that ended ten months later. My heart was bruised, but I stepped back and took a long, difficult inventory of my life. I had a tendency to silence myself, to become invisible, adapting to the other person and their needs. All my life other people had defined me, saying I was smart, shy, super responsible, and that I lived in my head. I believed them, and molded myself to become that person. I assumed others knew me better than I knew myself. Mark helped awaken something inside of me, which was the knowledge that I was capable of feeling deeply and that I had opinions of my own. It was time to start showing up, stop worrying about whether or not I'd find the perfect person, and be completely myself.

Shortly after my breakup with Mark, I flew to France to spend Christmas with my friends Synthiea and Dimitri. It was a magical time, walking though the open-air market at night drinking mulled wine as the snow fell lightly all around us. I was welcomed and comforted in their home and I felt myself healing. Lulled by the beauty all around me, I was convinced by Synthiea to sign up for Match.com. I was curious to see whom I might meet, but after several coffee dates and a very brief relationship, I became disillusioned with the process. I realized that I had amazing friends, great kids, and work I loved that would support me financially. My grandparents had instilled in me a passion for travel and I knew I would continue to find ways to have all the adventures I wanted. I didn't need to be in a relationship to realize my dreams. I actually was very content with my life, and so, after my brief fling with online dating, I deactivated my profile.

Stability and consistency were the hallmarks of Terry's childhood. He grew up on a farm in northwestern Ohio where unpredictability came with the weather, not family, friends, or community. During the school year he attended classes, participated in after-school activities such as band or cross-country, and went home to work in the fields. He learned to drive a tractor at five, and as he got older he took on more challenging tasks helping his father around the farm. After graduating from high school, he followed in his older brother's footsteps, attending a local Christian college, assuming he'd become a teacher and return to his hometown to settle down.

It didn't take long for Terry to figure out that college and the life of a math teacher were not for him. He had no passion for classes, homework, or conforming, and he couldn't connect what he liked learning with the endless requirements unrelated to his interests. After two years of trying to make it work, he dropped out of school without any idea of what he'd do next. He urgently needed to find a way to support himself and had no desire to return to the farm or farming. Seeing the advertisement "Join the Navy, See the World", he investigated further, and when he discovered they'd give him not only food, lodging, and clothing, but a paycheck, he enlisted on the spot.

Life onboard ship was interesting but isolating. To ease his loneliness, Terry corresponded with a woman he knew from high school. They dated when he was home on leave and shared the same values of family and faith. They took a few motorcycle rides, and went out dancing and partying with friends, and it seemed to Terry she was as interested in adventures and activities as he was. She was cute, he was in love, and, while still at sea, he asked her to marry him. After his enlistment ended they settled in California, where their children, Aaron and Jessica, were born.

Terry took correspondence classes and found he learned best when he could work at his own pace and with real problems to solve. He studied electronics while onboard ship, and once out in the working world he taught himself computer programming. In the early 'nineties, on a whim, Terry applied for a job with a fast-growing, exciting company looking for talented software developers. When his friends joked that Microsoft would never hire someone his age, forty, he replied, "Well, I already don't have a job there, so what do I have to lose if they say no?" The family soon moved to Seattle.

They settled into a comfortable life centered on family, work, and church, but as the kids left for college Terry struggled with his marriage. There were underlying tensions that for years he believed were his responsibility to repair. Stepping out of the role of fixer, he felt an emptiness and a longing for a deeper connection. Terry had entered the relationship as himself, but over the years he had retreated more and more, slowly becoming invisible. He married someone he thought shared his sense of passion and adventure, but he no longer believed she did. Unable to find a way to feel comfortable and safe expressing his true feelings, he decided he'd rather be alone and filed for divorce. He moved out of his home and felt contentment with the solitude and quiet he experienced.

Going through the transition, he asked a friend for advice. His friend recommended getting counseling, which he did. One day he mentioned to his therapist that for the first time in years he had noticed a woman while shopping at the supermarket, and thought she was attractive. Up until that time he hadn't been thinking about dating, but when his therapist suggested that maybe he was ready to try, she also told him to take his time and not get serious about anyone for at least a year. Terry had been out of circulation for the past twenty-six years and had no idea how to meet people in the digital age. Co-workers suggested posting a profile on Match.com. He spent several days pondering what to write, finally came up with something, and with a great deal of trepidation, hit "submit."

And that is when I opened an email from Match.com that said, "Here are ten people who fit your profile." I hadn't been active online for a few months, and I have no idea why, on that particular day, I opened the file. I have even less of an idea why

I chose to look at "Aivomot." His was not the most handsome photo, and his user name was odd. However, as I read his profile I was intrigued. He seemed unpretentious, honest, and interesting. The books he listed were some I had just finished reading. He wrote about hiking, wine tasting, motorcycling, and skiing, and that for now he was seeking only friendships. He wanted someone to do things with, and if it became something more, that was fine, as long as it evolved naturally.

Finding nothing to warn me away, I wrote him a brief note, and his response was quick and positive, unusual for the online dating world. We exchanged emails back and forth, often several a day. In one particularly amusing exchange, we shared what we now call our "scar" stories. I was recovering from a broken arm, which I had injured skiing six weeks earlier. He was adjusting to life without basketball due to plantar fasciitis. I wrote about my own plantar fascia injury the prior fall. He said our exchanges reminded him of a scene in one of the *Lethal Weapon* movies where Mel Gibson and Rene Russo are comparing battle wounds.

We both liked the ease of our conversations and the lack of game playing. Because of my work and the possibility of clients recognizing my profile, I hadn't posted a picture of me online, and I offered to send one to Terry when we first began writing. For some reason the attachment with my photo never went through, but rather than have me try again, he told me it was actually fine. He was a bit surprised to realize the experience of writing and learning about each other was more important than worrying about what I looked like. He earned a lot of brownie points for that answer.

I kept my hopes in check. I had previously shared a fairly lengthy email exchange with someone and I was anticipating we'd hit it off when we finally met. The man who showed up for that dinner was not the one I had known online—he was nice, quiet, and relatively uninteresting. I was disappointed, but I also learned a valuable lesson—writing clever emails for weeks couldn't tell what meeting someone in person could in just a few minutes. I wanted to find out what Terry was really like, and I wanted to know if we had even a hint of connection. So after only six days of correspondence we arranged to have dinner together one evening after work. Chris, my son, had been visiting his sister Katie in New York, and his flight was scheduled to land that night at midnight. I had time to kill and proposed we get the awkward first encounter out of the way.

Picking a location where I'd feel safe and was easy for both of us to find, I chose the Cheesecake Factory at a local shopping mall. Arriving first, I knew I would recognize Terry since I had seen his pictures in his online profile. He had no idea what I looked like, so when he walked into the restaurant, I approached him and said hi. I was pleasantly surprised. He looked much nicer than his photograph, and was very casual and friendly. He later told me he had some fear that I'd take one look at him, walk right past him out the door, and he'd never know.

After a long day of listening to clients I'm either very talkative or else worn out and quiet. I had warned Terry I wasn't sure which Lynda would show up. It was definitely talkative Lynda who was there that night, and four hours flew by. We fell into an easy conversation. My experience working with couples led me to ask him some pointed questions right at the start, knowing his answers could determine whether it was worth pursuing anything further. We discussed religion, something he mentioned in his profile. He's a Christian, I'm a Unitarian. I wanted to know if our differing beliefs would be a barrier. I asked him another direct question about his feelings regarding homosexuality. Chris is gay and I would never tolerate being in a relationship with someone who wasn't completely comfortable with him. Terry told me the story of his son Aaron's conversion to Judaism, and his belief that there were many paths we all take in this world. His answers were very open and nonjudgmental, and I felt myself relax. He asked me what I liked about traveling, and we both felt a shiver of excitement when our descriptions of loving the journey, not the destination, were so similar. In all the topics we discussed, no red flags appeared for either of us.

Midway through our evening Terry asked if he could move to my side of the table to remove the physical barrier between us. Sitting next to each other felt surprisingly normal and comfortable. As the time for me to leave approached, Terry asked me what my plans were for the following Sunday.

"I'm walking with my friend Laura at one, I need to do laundry, I have to fix dinner for Chris," I said as I pictured my schedule out loud.

"I need to wash my hair," is what he heard.

He stopped my rambling with, "Help me here, I'm trying to ask you out."

I realized he just needed me to say yes, let's go on a date. "Yes," I answered.

Terry walked me to my car in the mall parking lot. On the way we passed by his motorcycle and stopped to chat while he put on his protective gear. Impulsively, he gave me a hug before we parted. He called me the next day and told me his first reaction was embarrassment, and he thought he should apologize for his action. But then he decided no, this was who he was and if it wasn't OK with me, then maybe I wouldn't be the right person for him to date. This was our first experience of what we came to call "flinches", reactions to previous relationships that did not necessarily fit into ours but kept showing up. I told Terry I thought the hug felt very natural and nice.

CHAPTER TWO

Motorcycles

My first encounter with a motorcycle was when I was eleven. My mother's second husband, Jim, had been an amateur stock-car racer before they married. He loved to speed on the open highway, and sometimes took us on trips into the mountains where he could practice cornering with our brand new front-wheel-drive Olds Toronado. One day he came home with a small motorbike and offered to take me for a ride—no helmet, boots, or gloves, just shorts and a T-shirt as we cruised through the neighborhood. We were having a great time until we turned up our short, steep, driveway. Mistaking the clutch for the brake, he crashed the front wheel into the garage door. I emerged relatively unscathed, with only a minor sprain to my little finger, but my tears and my flair for the dramatic alarmed my mother. That was it, no more riding for me, motorcycles were far too dangerous. The bike quickly disappeared and I have no idea what happened to it.

During my freshman year of high school, one of my friends, Gil, showed up at our house riding a small Honda 50cc motorcycle. My stepsister Karen and I were impressed because most of our friends weren't driving cars yet, let alone a motorcycle. Even cooler, Gil took me for rides up and down the streets of the neighborhood without my parents' knowledge. Karen wasn't interested, but I was and Gil taught me how to ride. I was a quick study, and loved the feeling of steering the machine, shifting gears, and, of course, doing something behind my mom's back. A few years later Gil became my first biker friend when he rebuilt a Harley-Davidson and had a python tattooed around his upper arm. But once cars entered my world, motorcycles faded away in my rearview mirror.

Terry was introduced to motorcycling in 1976 by John, a friend from Ohio, also in the Navy and coincidentally stationed in California. They reconnected when both their ships were in dry dock in Long Beach. He gave Terry a few rides on the back of his motorcycle and Terry thought the bike was a lot of fun as well as a relatively cheap form of transportation. Taking out a loan, he bought a new Honda CB550K. It was a middleweight motorcycle capable of freeway speeds but not too heavy or powerful for a new rider.

The salesman gave Terry his entire motorcycle safety course— "Here's the clutch lever, here's the brake lever, this is the throttle, and here are the turn signals." His training complete, Terry pulled out of the dealership onto the busy streets of Long Beach and learned how to ride. A few months later he rode to Ohio with another Navy friend who was on a Kawasaki KZ400, a bike with a much smaller engine that could barely keep up with Terry's at freeway speeds. Terry had to repeatedly slow down and wait for him. After his marriage, Terry bought a larger Honda CB750F, which could more easily handle a rider and passenger. He and his wife rode from Long Beach to Ohio and back, stopping often to take breaks and sightsee. Terry loved the ride, but had to wear a kidney belt to cope with the vibration from the bike's primitive suspension.

Married, starting a family, and needing a second car, Terry sold the bike. It wasn't until Aaron entered college and his daughter was in high school that his long-dormant passion for riding was reawakened. When he took Jessica to the Department of Licensing for her driver's permit, he impulsively took the motorcycle written test, reading the instructional booklet while he stood in line. Soon after, curious to see if Harley-Davidson motorcycles had evolved over the years, he sat on one in a local showroom. He realized he wasn't interested when all it brought back were memories of his Navy days and the discomfort his friends experienced riding Harleys. Driving past a BMW motorcycle dealer, he stopped to check out their bikes. This time he took a test ride and was impressed with the technology, suspension, and handling. One week later, he came home with a new BMW R1100RT, a cross between a sportbike, capable of handling corners and quick turns, and a touring bike, designed for comfort over long distances.

Terry began riding to and from work, and took short day rides with his wife as he became more comfortable carrying a passenger. His interest in long-distance riding was piqued when he heard George Barnes speak at a meeting of the BMW Motorcycle Owners of America in Redmond, Oregon. George was a member of the Iron Butt Association, and he was also the winner of the 1999 Iron Butt Rally, an eleven-day, eleven-thousand-mile endurance event put on by the IBA. George explained that the Iron Butt Association was an organization for motorcyclists interested in long-distance riding who completed a certified ride to qualify for membership. The most common ride was called a SaddleSore, and involved riding 1000 miles in less than 24 hours and documenting it using gas receipts and witness forms for both the start and finish of the ride.

Shortly after George's talk Terry had to go to Cincinnati for a work-related conference and decided to ride his motorcycle. He calculated that the distance would qualify as a SaddleSore and give him his first Iron Butt Association certified ride. He read various pieces of advice and planned the details. Several riders suggested beginning a ride at midnight so the latter part of the ride, when he'd be the most tired, would take place in daylight. He soon realized his mistake when he had to stop twice for naps at rest areas, exhausted. It was too much of a disruption to his normal sleep pattern. Finally, after about twenty hours, he hit the 1000-mile mark and found a hotel room.

Awakening a few hours later, he continued his ride to Cincinnati, satisfied with the SaddleSore. But over the next several hundred miles, as he checked his odometer and his watch, he realized he could complete a different IBA ride, the Bun Burner, which is 1500 miles in 36 hours. He had the necessary paperwork with him, so when he reached the 1500-mile mark in North Platte, Nebraska, all he had to do was find witnesses to vouch that he had been there. He returned to work the following week and turned in his expense report requesting reimbursement for over 4800 miles. His manager was dumbfounded and had no idea how to respond—most employees flew to conferences.

I knew motorcycling was Terry's great passion. For us to move much further in any relationship I needed to discover for myself if I liked motorcycling as an activity on its own merits or simply because I liked Terry. I knew if I only did it for him I might tire of it someday, which would become a source of conflict instead of a shared interest. On our third date I asked him if he would take me out on the bike. He loaned me protective gear from his collection of jackets and pants. I wore his old helmet, which fit me well enough, and a pair of my leather boots. He got on the bike first, then showed me how to get on behind him, balancing myself by holding on to his shoulder as he planted his feet and leaned forward. Awkwardly, I climbed onto the bike and settled onto the seat. I must have looked quite stylish as I kept cinching up his several-sizes-too-big pants so they wouldn't fall off of me.

Terry explained how to be a pillion, or passenger, which meant doing nothing, letting the bike dictate whether I leaned or stayed upright. My job was to be "invisible" so I wouldn't make any sudden moves to disrupt the balance of the bike, creating a problem for him. We headed out on a favorite route of his, combining twisting suburban roads with quiet country lanes. As I relaxed I found myself being gently pulled into leaning along with the bike, with no effort on my part, when it went around corners. I thought I might be nervous, but instead I enjoyed the feeling of being in the open air and checking out the scenery. When we rode by a field with manure piled high, ready for spring planting, I was surprised how much the smell overpowered me. Riding in a car blocks so many sensations, but sitting on the back of the bike I was enveloped in them. Even though they weren't all pleasant sights or smells, it felt so much more engaging than experiencing them through the narrow confines of a car window. We stopped for gas about halfway through the ride and he asked me if I was having fun. I told him it was a good thing the helmet had a visor or I would have had to pick the bugs out of my teeth from grinning so widely.

A few weeks after that first ride, on one of our hiking dates, we lost the trail in the snow, missed a turn, and conquered a completely different summit. We collapsed, exhausted, and began laughing at our predicament. As we sat in the warm sunshine, surrounded by trees and mountains, Terry began to speak of our relationship and how it was becoming more than casual dating. Instead of elated, I was terrified. While I wasn't sure how I felt about Terry, I knew I wanted to keep seeing him. But I had also come to a place of contentment with my life, and I was cautious about getting too close too soon, moving too quickly, and then finding out we really weren't a good match for each other. I wanted to take things slowly, to spend time talking, sharing, and getting to know each other, before deciding if I really wanted to bring anyone into my life. When I met Terry I had finally found my voice, and I wanted to be certain I could hold out for what I really valued before committing to anything more serious.

Also, I was only the second person he had dated after ending his marriage, and I wanted to make sure I wasn't the "rebound girl." Did he really know me? Was he falling for an image in his own mind? I asked him if he thought he needed to date others, to sow his wild oats after being in a relationship for twenty-six years. He told me the advice he got from his brother about dating— when you meet the right person, you'll know. Terry had dated a lot prior to his wedding, and he liked the idea of marriage. His relationship hadn't ended because he wanted freedom, but because for him it was dysfunctional and he had lost faith that it could ever be repaired.

I needed more time, and said we needed to go slowly and let things happen naturally. I had to face my anxiety of being hurt again, to let down my barriers, and trust that I could be myself and love someone else. I wanted to make sure he was the right person, and that I wasn't just responding to his feelings for me. Over the next few days, as I sat with my fears and my questions, I realized he understood me in a way no one ever had before, and had shown no hesitation in knowing I was the right person for him. I felt myself surrendering, letting go of control. I found myself willing to trust Terry not only with my well-being, but with my heart.

Spring was still in the air as we went for another ride. Meandering alongside a river carving its way through a beautiful canyon, I realized how natural the bike was becoming for me, the ease with which I now hopped on and off, no longer thinking about how to strap on my helmet or hook up the intercom. I also recognized how natural my relationship with Terry felt, and the ease of being myself around him. Stopping for lunch, as we relaxed on a boulder and listened to the chatter of our friends and the rushing of the river all around us, I told Terry I, too, had fallen in love.

Terry had a longer day ride he liked to take when the snow melted and the roads were clear. It started in the Snoqualmie Valley, along a meandering road through horse fields and farms, and slowly climbed up the western side of the Cascades. The air was crisp and the trees were beginning to leaf out. It was a gorgeous day and we were joined by a few of our friends. The views were spectacular. Snow still clung to the mountainsides as we stopped for a break at the top of Stevens Pass before descending the eastern side, riding alongside a river raging as it thundered its way over rocks and waterfalls. I relaxed into the rhythm of the bike as I took it all in. Stopping for lunch in Leavenworth, I enjoyed the camaraderie, food, and conversations. Back on the bike, we wove through Bluett Pass, with its sweeping turns eventually giving way to open fields, before turning west again towards Snoqualmie Pass and home.

As we rode that day, I let my mind wander, taking in what it was I was experiencing and why I was enjoying it so much. A hiker and skier by nature, I like speed and being outdoors. Riding behind Terry I felt the movement of the bike and the rush of the wind going by me. I was immersed in the sights and smells all around me, and I was going somewhere, even if it was just over the next hill. I was sharing the same space, enjoying the same adventure, with someone with whom I had fallen in love. When I asked Terry to take me for that first ride, I needed to know if motorcycling would someday come between us. I now had nothing to fear, because motorcycling was already becoming interwoven into the life we were building together.

CHAPTER THREE

Sure, Why Not?

It was clear motorcycles would be a major part of our time together, but Terry didn't just ride for a few hours now and then. His true passion was long-distance riding, something I knew nothing about and, even after he explained it to me, had no interest in. Riding endless hours, day after day, seemed to border on crazy. Terry was exploring other forms of endurance, most notably running, and was training for his first half marathon. In one of our earliest conversations he asked if I had ever considered running a 13.1-mile race and I laughed out loud. Not only did I have no interest in such a thing, it wasn't even part of my vocabulary.

Spending quiet time alone in his head was natural for him. He grew up on a farm where he spent hours by himself on a tractor. He had completed numerous Iron Butt certified rides and he enjoyed solitude. Terry had also always been a runner, starting with the cross-country team in high school. When he began working out with a personal trainer during his divorce she asked him to describe his fitness routine. He said he'd been running six to eight miles at a time, several times a week, for the past few months. Surprised at how easily he could run those distances, she encouraged him to try a half marathon and he accepted her challenge.

I, on the other hand, was a social being with a fairly short attention span. I loved trying new things, hanging out with friends, and acting on the spur of the moment. I grew up before the era of Title IX, when most girls stopped doing sports once we were no longer forced to run laps in high school. I played touch football and was the star of the kickball team in elementary school, but once I hit junior high it was no longer cool to be athletic. In college I hiked and camped, and during my marriage I climbed and backpacked. I joined my family in studying karate and earned my brown belt before deciding my heart wasn't in it. When my kids were in middle school and high school, I played tennis and moved up through the ranks on a competitive club team. Tennis met a social need and reminded me of the fun I had had as a young girl participating in playground sports.

I had slowly added working out to my routine but it was only after a foot injury temporarily sidelined my tennis game that I began taking it seriously. Once my foot healed I began working with Kim, a personal trainer. She added running to vary my aerobic conditioning, but it was limited to at most three miles on a treadmill and a lot of complaining on my part. Kim encouraged me to attempt my first outdoor run, Seattle's annual St. Pat's Dash, a 3.5-mile "race" with thousands of people and a beer garden at the end. It was hardly a contender for long-distance running but I had a fantastic time. Still, when Terry asked me to join him for the half marathon I thought to myself that running that far was crazy. I chose instead to be the cheerleader and greet him at the finish line.

In 2004, when we'd been dating barely a month, Terry competed in The Waltz Across Texas, a twenty-four-hour long-distance motorcycle rally. This was the first I had ever heard of a rally. He explained that there were two different types. One, which most people think of when they think of motorcycles, is a social gathering such as Sturgis, where thousands of Harley-Davidson riders descend on Sturgis, South Dakota, to share stories, check out vendor booths, and party heartily with friends. Honda and BMW associations hold more sedate annual rallies where riders often camp out, dealers show off new motorcycles, and awards are given to members for accomplishments such as the most miles ridden in a year.

The other type of rally is more like a scavenger hunt, and appeals to those who prefer solitude and endurance riding. They usually last twenty-four to thirty-two hours, and represent a small subculture in the wider world of motorcycling. There are a variety of formats, but most involve a list of locations, called bonuses, where the rider has to do something such as take a picture or answer a question. Terry had been to a few of the BMW Motorcycle Owners of America rallies and enjoyed them, but he was much more interested in the long-distance events. The Waltz was his second endurance rally after his first, the Utah 1088, the previous June.

Terry told me about his Utah rally to help me understand what he would be dealing with in Texas. In the 2003 1088 he rode solo and did all his planning alone. Each rider was given a list of bonuses with one main route and several optional routes. Each bonus had a point value, some higher than others. The rider who collected the highest number of points won. Most participants followed the main route and tried to get as many bonuses along the way as they could. After exploring all the options, Terry decided to follow the main route.

He spent most of the daylight hours locating and photographing bonuses, enjoying the riding and the experience of trying to find the things listed in his rally packet. In the late afternoon he came upon two riders, one of who had just collided with a deer and literally split it in half. Miraculously, the rider, covered in animal blood and guts, had kept the bike upright until he came to a stop. The motorcycle was now sitting on the side of the road awaiting a tow truck. Terry stopped to confirm the rider was fine, and that help was on the way, and took off again. He arrived at the checkpoint later that night hungry and exhausted. He sat down for what he thought would be a short rest, and woke up almost an hour later. Getting back on the bike, he pulled onto the freeway before realizing he was headed in the wrong direction for the next bonus. He struggled to figure out where he was, and now wanted only to finish the rally and get back to the hotel. He bypassed several easy bonuses so he could simply accumulate the minimum mileage to be classified as a finisher. While the 1088 had been brutal in many respects, Terry enjoyed the experience enough that he wanted to compete in more rallies. He'd heard The Waltz Across Texas was an excellent rally, and since it took place early in the spring, it would give him more practice before trying another one that summer in Utah.

I was in Arizona visiting friends while he rode his bike from Washington to Texas, and we chatted daily on the phone. One night he called from a restaurant in a remote town and told me he had shared his table with two women. He said he felt uncomfortable having the conversation with me but saw this as an opportunity for him to be completely himself and not fear repercussions. We both knew these women were no threat, that he was just being friendly. This was really a conversation about transparency, about how important it was to never keep secrets. The threat would be if we ever felt afraid to share our lives fully and started to hide innocuous things. If we allowed shadows to creep into our relationship it would destroy trust. Trust was essential for both of us, and without really discussing it, we somehow knew we were creating something very important.

Terry and I had talked about everything from the very beginning, never hiding any of the darker aspects of our pasts or ourselves. Following our second date, when it was clear we were interested in continuing to see each other, he sat me down and shared some very personal issues in both his past and his present situation. I listened carefully, and appreciated his honesty and the difficulty he had in opening up painful places in his life. I told him my stories, the ones I usually kept from others. Rather than driving us apart, these conversations brought us closer, and our vulnerability created a stronger connection.

The Waltz Across Texas Rally was a lot of fun for Terry, although he again struggled with routing challenges. His GPS unit often sent him off on weird roads or in the wrong direction, and his lack of knowledge of the geography of Texas was a definite limitation. He had no one with whom to share his frustrations or talk over decisions, and he was still very much a novice. Overall he was pleased to finish the Rally, and that whetted his appetite for Utah. He also met Jim Owen, a highly respected long-distance rider. Jim had recently married, and he and Terry shared a bond as they exchanged stories about the women who had come into their lives.

Terry got home from Texas with a speeding ticket for a souvenir because he was in such a hurry to see me again—it was clear our relationship was progressing. We spent most of our time together, and it was beginning to feel odd when we were apart. Prior to meeting me, Terry signed up for his second Utah 1088 rally. After we had been dating awhile, he asked me if I'd like to fly to Utah to be in Salt Lake City for the finish, which sounded like fun. As the time got closer, I asked him whether it made sense for me to ride with him to Utah and just hang out while he rode the rally. But that meant he couldn't use the auxiliary fuel cell that solo riders use to carry extra gas and minimize fuel stops. It was attached to the bike in place of the passenger seat, so if we rode to Utah together, how would he get the tank there?

Innocently, I asked, "What if we rode the rally together?"

What started as a seemingly simple question became a pivotal conversation in our relationship. I was surprised that I was even considering riding in a rally. I knew it wasn't coming from anything Terry had said, or any pressure I was feeling. I was intrigued by what he was doing, and I was becoming less interested in standing on the sidelines, waving goodbye as he rode off. I wanted to explore what it might feel like to be a participant and share the same experiences he was having. At the same time, I was intimidated and wanted to understand what I was even considering before committing to anything.

I needed to ask important questions and listen to Terry's answers instead of assuming I knew what he thought. It was important for me to voice my fears and concerns. The discussion centered on riding, but it really was about who we were and how we looked at the world. Pete, my ex, did everything with such intensity that I couldn't find a way to connect with him. My style was more relaxed, more focused on the sharing. Terry talked about his ex-wife and his experiences in his marriage. To him, it felt that not only did she not appreciate his passion for adventure, but in many ways resented it. We both wanted a partner with whom we could experience life together, without feeling like we were either being dragged along or forcing the other into something they didn't enjoy. I was secretly terrified that Terry's desire to rally was only about winning. I knew I wouldn't want to, or be able to, share that with him. I'm a very competitive person, but my desire to compete has more to do with bettering myself than winning medals.

"Why do you ride in rallies?" I asked Terry. "What are your goals? Is this an individual dream of yours? Is there room to share? Can you imagine us riding for all those hours on the same bike? What might it be like to compete together?"

His answers in some ways surprised me, and in others fit the man I was coming to know. "I like the challenge of riding, of figuring out a route, seeing if I can execute it, and being with other riders who share my passion," he said. "Winning is fun, but not at the expense of the experience."

I talked about my fears that I'd be pressured to do more than I felt comfortable doing, and disappoint him if I couldn't keep up. He talked about the excitement of having me along, and was thrilled I'd even consider riding with him. He valued my company and wanted me to share the experience of the rally with him. We recognized we were committed to building a relationship based on being together, and the logical outcome of that was to try riding a rally as a team. I think we were both surprised to find ourselves agreeing to attempt tackling the 1088. We agreed that we'd put "us" ahead of any competition. We'd quit before we did any emotional damage to either one of us. Our number one goal was to have fun.

The half marathon had consumed most of his time and energy since his return from Texas, and our longest ride together had been our three-pass, 250-mile day trip almost two months earlier. Terry wanted to make sure both of us could do the 1100-plus miles necessary to complete the rally, as well as the 840 miles each way to and from Salt Lake City. He felt very strongly that we should ride a SaddleSore together, but there was one minor problem. The Utah 1088 was a week and a half away, and we'd need to leave the following Wednesday for Salt Lake City. The only time we had left to do the ride was in two days, over the upcoming weekend.

Not fully understanding how crazy this was, I said sure, and we planned our ride. Three of our friends, Kevin, Lisa, and Jake, were going to ride over Lolo Pass, a mountain highway through Idaho and Montana, and camp along the way. They invited us to come along as far as they were going and then take off on our own. Another rider, Bruce, was also attempting a SaddleSore. We would be the only ones riding two-up—two people on the same motorcycle. Terry, who had always wanted to ride Lolo Pass, and I, not knowing any better, agreed. At the last minute a sixth friend, Doru, asked to tag along on a Yamaha R1, a sportbike designed for high speed over short distances. His plan was to ride with us for a few hundred miles and then turn back.

CHAPTER FOUR

Endurance

M ost first-time SaddleSores are done on long stretches of interstate, where it's easy to keep a good, steady pace and the wear and tear of riding is kept to a minimum by using cruise control. Terry told me it's actually quite easy to finish a SaddleSore in about eighteen hours of riding time, and we could do it if we didn't waste much time at stops. It wasn't necessary to speed, and in fact, going too fast just wears out the rider. Most riders do these rides solo, or at most with one other person so they can set their own pace. Not only was our route over Lolo Pass, famous for its "Twisty Road Next 77 Miles" sign, but we were riding with a group of people with differing agendas.

Things got interesting early on. We stopped for lunch in Colfax, Washington, about 250 miles from our start. All six bikes were parked in a line, ours second from the end. While we were eating we heard a huge crash and ran over to find our bike on its side and a young man sprawled on the ground next to his Stingray bicycle. He had tried to ride between two of our bikes, maybe to snag my jacket off the seat or just show off. He clipped the motorcycle as he passed and knocked it off the sidestand. Our windscreen hit Kevin's footpeg, cracking off a third of the side of our screen. We called the local police, who recognized the punk as a local troublemaker. This, of course, did not bode well for holding him accountable for damages.

It took a full hour to finish the police business while the clock ticked away on our SaddleSore. We called a BMW dealer in another town to get a new windscreen but it wasn't open. Reluctantly, Terry told me our ride was over, that we needed to head home to get the screen repaired. I almost went crazy. There had to be some way we could keep going. I was so determined to complete the SaddleSore that I refused to consider quitting. Encouraged by my stubbornness, the group solved the problem with the motorcyclist's friend, duct tape. Layer upon layer of it patched the screen up well enough for us to continue.

Lolo Pass was gorgeous, filled with long sweeping turns for the advertised seventy-seven miles, with hills rising up on one side of the road and a rushing river on the other. My body moved in concert with the motorcycle, and my mind was occupied with the beauty all around me. I also got a first-hand understanding of why it's hard to ride with a group. The other riders needed to stop, and never at the same intervals. Jake was a smoker who took longer breaks than we needed, someone else needed a pit stop, a third was hungry. It was hard for a group to keep up with one another as we passed cars and slow-moving RVs. Reaching the campground at the top of the pass, we said our goodbyes to Lisa, Kevin, and Jake, and continued on with Bruce and Doru. Doru, our "only going for a short ride" rider, couldn't seem to stop. Our plan was to ride east just beyond Missoula to Drummond, Montana, to make sure we would have enough miles for the SaddleSore, then turn west back towards Seattle. Arriving in

Drummond, we had a quick bite to eat and the four of us parted ways. We later found out Doru completed an undocumented SaddleSore. I have no idea how long it took him to walk upright again.

*Encouraged by my stubbornness, the group solved
the problem with duct tape.*

Terry and I were finally on our own. Nearing Moses Lake in eastern Washington around 2 a.m., Terry kept shaking his head to fight off exhaustion. I fed him pieces of lemon candy, one of his strategies for staying awake. We turned up the music on his mini CD—Meat Loaf singing "Bat Out of Hell" at full volume, a song he told me almost always helped revive him. I talked to him to try to engage his mind, but he was struggling. He finally told me he needed to get off the road and stop riding.

Many long-distance riders sleep in what's called the Iron Butt Motel, slang for a picnic bench in a rest area or some other quiet, out-of-the-way location. They simply pull in, lie on the table in full gear, often leaving their helmets on, and pass out. Terry had described this method of catching a short nap to me before we started, but my anxiety about tweaking my back on a hard surface, and the unknown of sleeping in such strange circumstances, prompted me to make him promise a real bed surrounded by four walls. We tried to find a decent hotel near the freeway off-ramp in Moses Lake, but everything was full. Someone directed us into town where the only place we could find had bars on the windows and rented for $38 a night. Glad that it was dark outside and we didn't have to see how disgusting it really was, we took the last remaining room. We threw down our gear, plopped down on the bed, and immediately fell asleep.

Terry's normal habit in such circumstances was to sleep until he woke up spontaneously. I was so fixated on completing the SaddleSore that I begged him to set a timer for two hours to give us time to get back to our finish in Issaquah within the twenty-four-hour window. He said if he felt rested enough in two hours we could keep going. When our trucker's Screaming Meanie alarm clock ("Loud Enough to Wake the Dead!") beeped after what seemed like only minutes, Terry was wide awake and ready to go. With just twenty minutes to spare we made it back to our starting point and printed our final gas receipt as proof of our finish. I had passed my test with flying colors, and Terry still brags that he got me to stay in a $19-per-hour motel.

Back home, after trying to replace his specialty windscreen with the old stock one, Terry discovered that the RT was far more damaged than he had thought. The bike has a fairing that wraps around the front and sides for wind protection. The front fairing subframe, which included the brackets that raise and lower the windscreen, was bent. The original screen wouldn't fit no matter how Terry tried to tweak it. Checking over the rest of the bike he leaned lightly on one of the saddlebags and it unexpectedly broke away. One of the mounting brackets was gone and it couldn't be repaired without a new part. There was no way we could ride the RT to Utah in its current condition.

Luck was on our side, however, since Terry had a spare motorcycle, a 2003 BMW R1150 GS Adventure, sitting in the garage. It's a slightly taller motorcycle and it has less wind protection because it's a dual-sport, which means it can go both on paved roads and off-road on dirt and gravel. The passenger seat is smaller, and while it had a custom seat, it wasn't designed for my bottom. It also had a screw in one of the tires and wasn't ready for a 3000-mile ride. In June it's almost impossible to get into a BMW dealer for planned repairs let alone emergencies, but Terry called and begged the service manager to replace the tire for us so we could leave in two days for the rally. Feeling sorry for us, the dealer agreed to fix the tire. Terry asked him if he'd also throw in an oil change. The dealer agreed, but added, "Enough! That's it, don't press your luck!" as he hung up the phone.

CHAPTER FIVE

Sitting on the Curb

I'm not sure a SaddleSore prepares a novice for a twenty-six-hour rally. The only goal with a SaddleSore is to ride 1000 miles, on any road, in any direction, in under twenty-four hours. You have as long as you want to figure out the best route, get your gear ready, and get started. If you miss a start time you just punch the clock a bit later. If you fail you can always try again tomorrow. The greatest challenge is managing time. Resisting the temptation to dawdle while taking a food or fuel stop gets harder as the day progresses. If you're careful about minimizing breaks and keeping an eye on your average speed, it's easy to get a few hours sleep and still finish well within the twenty-four-hour limit.

A long-distance motorcycle rally requires the same time-management skills as a SaddleSore, along with a few more. It's essentially a scavenger hunt, with bonuses worth different point values depending on the degree of difficulty to get to the location either in terms of distance or road quality. Each rally is run by a Rally Master who plans, advertises, and oversees the entire event. They take great pride in creating interesting routes, along twisty mountain roads filled with animals at night, blistering deserts in the heat of the day, busy cities at rush hour, or small towns with excruciatingly slow speed limits—anything to make the ride challenging. The goal of a rally is to figure out the best way to get the most points while also, at least in the 1088, riding the minimum number of miles to be classified as a finisher.

Riders usually start from a single location, and at the same time. While everyone has the same options for bonus collecting, not all riders will choose the same ones. Every rider tries to create a route that will maximize the chance of accumulating the most points, so after the first bonus or two it's common to go several hours without seeing any of the other riders, and then randomly run into them over the duration of the event as paths cross and re-cross. The rally usually ends at a specific time and place, and arriving even a minute late can cause disqualification. The rules of all rallies also clearly state that if a rider is carrying a passenger, the passenger can never take the controls. Even if I knew how to ride, I couldn't switch places with Terry to give him a break.

We had never ridden together for an overnight trip other than the SaddleSore, when spare clothing wasn't needed. When Terry handed me the tiny canvas satchel that would carry all my gear and have to fit into the saddlebag along with some spare parts for the bike, I was startled at how little I could take. After I packed thermal clothing for riding at night, a pair of lightweight hiking pants, a T-shirt, flip-flops to wear around the hotel, and a small Ziploc bag for toiletries, the satchel was just about full. There was no room for a second shirt or spare anything. I wore bike shorts and a running shirt under my outer protective gear. I insisted on at least bringing my makeup.

We rode the first 250 miles to Utah on Wednesday night, stopping in Pendleton, Oregon, for sleep. A short five hours later, we were back on the road to finish the remaining 600 miles, arriving in Salt Lake City with just enough time to check in to the hotel and head over to Steve Chalmers's for his traditional pre-rally barbeque. Steve is the Rally Master, or as he is usually called, the Rally Bastard. The '04 Rally would be the 13th running of this annual event, held the last weekend of June when the days were at their longest. I'd known Terry only three months, and because I was new to the sport I felt intimidated meeting all the riders, although it was a very pleasant surprise to be introduced to Jim and Diane Owen. This was the same Jim Owen that Terry met at The Waltz Across Texas. Diane would not be riding but came along as support.

Friday was technical inspection and odometer calibration, and the sixty or so other riders bustled around in the hotel parking lot. I had no idea what to expect and followed Terry around from station to station, turning in paperwork and having someone check out the bike. We then had to put on our gear and ride a set route to see how our odometer compared to a fixed mileage. Motorcycle odometers are notoriously unreliable, so an odometer check is used to determine exactly how many miles a rider covers in a rally. My job was to read the paperwork with the route on it to Terry while he rode us around. I felt nervous, afraid I'd make an error. Luckily the route was very simple, and we were quickly back at the hotel. Returning to our room to prepare for the next morning, we laid out all our gear, snacks, and maps for route planning. We headed off to dinner in the restaurant, and the riders' meeting afterwards.

Steve introduced himself and made it very clear his rules were the only rules. The clock on his cell phone was the only one that mattered for determining the finish time, and his say on scoring would be final. We wouldn't know the actual routes until the morning, but he did tell us there wouldn't be any tricks. Dirt roads would be identified and alternative routes would be available. Steve doesn't suffer fools gladly. Anyone who asked a decent question in the riders' meeting was rewarded with an honest answer, but anyone who asked what Steve considered a dumb question was rewarded with "the rock," which is just what it sounds like. The rock passed among quite a few riders. I kept my mouth shut.

I had never seen Terry anxious, or suspected how much difficulty he'd have sleeping the night before the start. He tossed and turned, replayed different scenarios in his mind, and worried we'd forget something or make a stupid mistake. When we finally woke up, he was tired, and I felt an urge to figure out a way to fix things, but there really wasn't anything for me to fix. I had to let it go and hope it didn't affect us later in the day.

We went to the riders' meeting at 6 a.m. to get our rally packs. The pack included a description of each bonus, what to do there, how to document it, and the times of the checkpoints. There were narrow time windows for the two checkpoints, and in this rally it was OK to miss one, but if you missed both you'd be disqualified. The Utah 1088, in those days, had a clearly defined base route, with turn-by-turn directions and milepost markers for bonuses, that was long enough to classify us as finishers. We could add bonuses, vary the route, or even take one of the alternative routes. Most bonuses were along the base route, but there were optional ones that were more challenging.

The official start was at 7 a.m., so we had one hour to come up with a route. We raced back to our room, pulled out our Utah map, and began planning. I had never seen a rally packet before, and it took me a few minutes to understand how it worked.

SOUTH US-191 TO JCT OF US-191/US-6

*****BONUS NUMBER 10 IS WORTH 510 POINTS (510) ON US-191, NEAR MP191, THERE IS AN INFORMATION SIGN POINTING TO A TOPOGRAPHICAL FEATURE ON YOUR RIGHT. WHAT IS THE NAME OF THE FEATURE THE SIGN IS TELLING IS ON YOUR RIGHT? THIS BONUS IS AVAILABLE AT ANY TIME DURING THE RALLY AND IS OPEN TO MAIN ROUTE RIDERS ONLY.

ANSWER _____ ODOMETER _____ TIME _____

*****BONUS NUMBER 11 IS WORTH 503 POINTS (503) ON US-191, AT MP177 IS A MILE MARKER SIGN. HOW MANY BOLTS HOLD THE 177 IN PLACE ON THE POST? THIS BONUS IS AVAILABLE AT ANY TIME DURING THE RALLY AND IS OPEN TO MAIN ROUTE RIDERS ONLY.

ANSWER _____ ODOMETER _____ TIME _____

The directions described the main route, but there were also extra bonuses thrown in randomly along the way. We needed to decide which ones to go after, and since it was my first rally I left all the decisions to Terry. He suggested we follow most of the set base route, which meant we essentially had to connect the dots, pick up bonuses along the way, read the instructions at least three times to make sure we met all the requirements, keep meticulous paperwork, and ride the miles. The route took us south during the heat of the day in temperatures above 100 degrees. Terry proposed modifying our route slightly to ride through Capital Reef National Park. We could pick up some extra bonuses, and he wanted me to see how beautiful it was. This allowed us to skip a bonus up Nine Mile Canyon, which was described as sixteen miles of dirt and gravel, likely too difficult for us riding two-up.

Digital cameras weren't widely used in rallies at the time because of problems downloading the different types of file cards, and the potential to cheat by altering the pictures. Instead, the rules said only Polaroid photos were accepted. Our camera was loaded and we had plenty of spare film. The rally package was in chronological order so following directions page by page was easy. We marked the bonus locations on our paper map as best we could, packed up our gear, and headed to the bike.

Riding the rally was much more entertaining than a SaddleSore. Having things to look for broke the miles into smaller segments and I felt engaged in a way I hadn't been before. I had a role, something to do instead of just sitting. As we approached a bonus, I read the instructions out loud so both of us understood what was expected. Once there I hopped off the bike, took the picture, and waited for it to develop to confirm it was correct.

I logged our time and odometer reading onto the pages of the rally pack, Terry put the photo into a Ziploc bag, and I got the packet ready for the next location. There were a few "drive-by" bonuses we could collect by simply slowing down and looking for the answer to a question on the bonus sheet—"At mile marker XYZ there is a sign with a suggested speed limit, what is it?" I jotted down the number, Terry read off the time and odo, and we were on our way again.

I had never been in southern Utah other than a brief stay in Zion years before, and the scenery was breathtaking. We rode through canyons and stunning rock landscapes. It was here I experienced my first bonus that involved getting off the bike and hiking.

***BONUS NUMBER 16 IS WORTH 2888 POINTS (2888) WE USED A VARIATION OF THIS BONUS IN 1995 WITH GREAT SUCCESS. . .WE'LL SEE HOW YOU FOLKS DO WITH THIS VERSION. TRAVEL WEST ON USH-24 FROM THE JCT OF USH95/USH-24. BETWEEN MP82 & MP81, ON YOUR RIGHT, WILL BE SIGNS FOR THE HICKMAN NATURAL BRIDGE. PARK YOUR SCOOTER AND FOLLOW THE TRAIL TOWARD HICKMAN BRIDGE. BETWEEN TRAIL MARKERS 5 & 6 WILL BE A SIGN TELLING YOU HOW FAR TO NAVAJO KNOBS. TAKE A PICTURE OF THAT SIGN. THIS BONUS IS AVAILABLE 24 HOURS, AND IS OPEN TO ALL RIDERS.

PICTURE _____ ODOMETER _____ TIME _____

Terry stayed with the bike to rest while I hiked up the trail. The skies were threatening to unload any minute, and if they did it would be a downpour. We debated what I should take with me and finally I took my protective outer jacket, a heavy, bulky load to drag along, and wore my outer pants. Rushing up the trail in motorcycle boots made the trip even more challenging, but I got the photograph, waited to make sure it developed correctly, and raced back to the bike before a single drop fell.

As the evening progressed another huge thunderstorm moved toward us from the west. We had just picked up a bonus of the "Welcome to Milford" sign and encountered a few guys who Terry assumed were at the tail end of the main route riders. They looked exhausted. Looking at our map and the next bonus on our list, Terry decided that 1000 points and riding into the storm wasn't worth the addition of an extra hundred miles and the wear and tear on him. He suggested turning north instead and rejoining the main route back in Delta.

The storm hit as we left Delta, and we rode in torrential rains for several hours. It was another first for me, learning that my protective gear, so hot and heavy in the heat of the day, was now a waterproof shield keeping me dry.

*****BONUS NUMBER 31 IS WORTH 289 POINTS (289) ON USH-36, BETWEEN MP53 & MP54, ON YOUR RIGHT IS THE CITY OF TOOELE'S FIRST CEMETERY. THERE ARE TWO MONUMENTS IN THE CEMETERY. WHEN WAS THE GRANITE MONUMENT NEAREST THE WOODEN WAGON ERECTED? THIS BONUS IS AVAILABLE 24 HOURS, AND IS OPEN TO ALL RIDERS.

ANSWER _____ ODOMETER _____ TIME _____

In Tooele we struggled to find the cemetery, and rode back and forth up the main street. We saw a few other riders obviously looking for the same bonus, also to no avail. We finally stopped at a gas station where I approached someone who looked like a local for help. He might have been more useful if his blood alcohol level had been slightly lower, or if I could have understood the words he was slurring, but somehow he got us pointed in the right direction. I soon found myself crawling up a hillside in the mud and slime into the cemetery where I located the monument and memorized the date. As I slid back down the slope towards the bike, I kept wondering what in the world I had gotten myself into, but I was amazed by how much fun I was having.

We spent the next several hours alone in the dark, fighting off the chill night air as we rode around the north side of the Great Salt Lake looking for bonuses, including a meditation center and a sign with the name of a ranch on it. Suddenly we were approached from behind by another couple who were obviously also riding the rally, and they slowed as they neared us. They, like us, had auxiliary lights on their bike. Long-distance riders usually add extra lights to supplement the stock headlights to help them see farther in the dark. For a while on the deserted two-lane highway we rode side by side with all our lights blazing, illuminating the entire skyline in front of us. I worried that a car might approach from the opposite direction and urged Terry to get behind the other bike. My thinking might have been distorted by exhaustion. Logically, any car coming toward us would see our lights miles away, and we would see theirs, and anyway it was doubtful many cars would even be on this road at this time of night.

After riding together awhile the other bike took off and we were again alone. I had a brief fright when Terry was surprised by the angle of a curve. Suddenly the bike leaned sharply toward the gravel edge alongside the asphalt, and it felt like we were about to slide off the road. I was pleased with my reaction, which was no reaction at all. I trusted my training to let the bike dictate what I should do and as we straightened back up Terry said it wasn't nearly as dramatic as it had seemed to me. He was confident in his ability to let the bike make the turn, and I was reminded how little experience I had on the bike and how much I still had to learn.

At my insistence, we pulled into a rest area at about 4 a.m. so I could take a much-needed break. My tailbone was killing me and I was exhausted. Terry signaled for me to get off the bike, but I couldn't move.

"You need to get off the bike," he said.

"I know," I replied.

"Well, then get off," he said.

"I can't remember what to tell my legs to do, and they have no idea what to do without my direction," was the only answer I could come up with.

It took a few minutes before I finally managed to stand, swing my leg over the seat, and find my balance on solid ground. I walked around a bit, dreading the idea of remounting. When it was time to get back on the bike my body rebelled and I almost didn't make it. I was exhausted, sore and miserable. I told Terry all I wanted to do was get back to the hotel, and I didn't care if we were finishers or not. I was fried and I couldn't believe he wasn't, too. For some reason, his lack of sleep the night before hadn't bothered him. He said the sun coming up always reinvigorated him, and he believed it would help me as well. I had my doubts, but I had fewer options. The only choice I really had was to head south on I-15, towards the hotel, on the bike.

As we rode along the west side of the Wasatch Mountains, the sun began to rise, slowly at first and then more rapidly. I felt a sense of hope returning and along with it my competitive spirit. There were two more bonuses on the way to the hotel, one near the airport and another at Temple Square in downtown Salt Lake City, and as we approached I told Terry I was now willing to get them. As I took each photo in the quiet of the early Sunday morning, I was glad I had listened to him and not made a hasty decision. I was also relieved to know that had I really needed to skip those final two he would have supported me and not been mad.

The final few miles! Turning west on I-80 towards the hotel, Terry said that because we had deviated from the main route, we might not have covered enough miles to be considered finishers. The possibility that we might be short on miles had never come up. We were well over what I thought was required, and I couldn't make any sense of his words. All I heard was, "We need to ride a billion miles past our exit, blah blah blah, then turn around and come on back." If I'd had the strength to strangle him, I would have. He later told me he could feel ice forming on the intercom wires from the sudden chill in my mood. I was in a state of utter disbelief, but Terry was insistent. I reluctantly agreed to go another twenty miles farther before turning around. I was not a happy camper when we passed by our exit and I could see the hotel from the interstate.

After what I considered a completely unnecessary detour we finally pulled into the hotel parking lot. We had ridden 1245 miles in just under twenty-six hours. I was amazed at the jumble of emotions I felt. I was grinning from ear to ear, laughing and crying at the same time. I couldn't believe what we had just accomplished. Steve Chalmers was the first to greet us and I think even he was surprised at my elation. As soon as we stopped the bike, a group of people gathered around the front of the GS, pointing and grabbing cameras. A large dragonfly had impaled itself on the grill, looking like some prehistoric masthead. The majesty of its pose seemed somehow symbolic of our accomplishment.

We finished up our paperwork and handed it in to be scored, then headed to our room for a shower and some badly needed sleep. The finishers' banquet, where the winners would be announced and we'd learn how well we did, was in a few hours and we wanted to be refreshed and ready to mingle with the other riders. The 1088 is, as far as I know, the only rally to have a separate category for couples. This year there were four couples entered, and I was pleased to just be a finisher. Imagine our surprise when we were called up as the third-place couple! To be fair, the fourth couple had been riding a great ride when a tire blew out on their bike. Fortunately, they were able to stop safely, but their rally was over. Had we been included in the overall rider placements, we would have finished approximately twenty-ninth out of fifty-six riders. Not bad for newbies, but more importantly I learned a beginner's lesson, and that is that first you have to finish.

Leaving for home early the next morning, Terry made it very clear that I should let him know when I needed a break. I had ridden over 3100 miles in the past week, condensed into essentially three intense twenty-four-hour periods, and I was facing another 850 miles back to Seattle. My tailbone was still sore from the rally, and I needed more frequent stops than he was used to. When we pulled into a gas station in Kennewick, Washington, about 200 miles from home, I asked to linger for a bit.

Terry became uncharacteristically irritated and abrupt. "We need to get going."

"Oh great, the honeymoon is over, here's the real Terry," I thought, and I became quiet and withdrawn.

He noticed my silence. "What's wrong?" he asked.

I resisted the urge to tell him, "Nothing," or to try and make it all better. This was an opportunity to really let him know what I was feeling and see how he responded. Was he really a jerk and I had been fooled, or was he the considerate man with whom I had fallen in love? I was sad and scared, and I forced myself to be honest.

"You're giving me mixed messages. You told me to tell you if I needed a break, and then you were upset when I did. I don't know what you want me to do, and I don't know which statement of yours to believe. It doesn't feel fair."

He was quiet as we got back on the bike and headed for home. There was an uncomfortable silence between us. A few miles later, he came on the intercom. "You're right, I did give you a mixed message. Here's the clear message—if you need to stop, we can stop and it's OK. Your comfort is more important than any imagined schedule. I'm not even sure why I thought we had to be on one. Let's quit riding for the night and you can take a rest."

While not completely relieved, I felt a bit better. We mutually made the decision to stop in Yakima, a mere 150 miles from home. After checking in, we sat on the steps outside the hotel and talked for well over an hour. We revisited our conversations about what was important to each of us, who we were, and what we each wanted in life. It was important for me to bring up all of my concerns, to really feel like Terry heard me. I didn't want to be in a relationship where I was promised one thing and given another. I wanted to feel safe expressing my needs, and have them taken seriously. Pete had often been dismissive of my fears, and I didn't want to be with someone again who did the same thing. Terry was used to being a caretaker, but sometimes felt like he was put in the position of having to make all the decisions in his marriage. He then felt blamed when things went wrong or the unexpected happened. He was still reactive to any hint of criticism, so when I first told him how I felt, he wasn't sure how to respond.

As we talked, the depth of our past experiences, and their impacts on us, became clear. But we handled it differently than either of us had been able to before. We talked deeply and honestly about ourselves and each other. We were open and vulnerable. Neither one of us raised our voice. This wasn't a fight, an argument, or even harsh words. Terry listened to me and said he was sorry. I told him how I felt without blame or anger. This was a major turning point in our relationship. We had our first serious misunderstanding, and we successfully navigated our way through it. "Sitting on the curb" became the template for all future conversations.

CHAPTER SIX

Blending

Motorcycling was becoming an important part of our time together, but our relationship was growing in other ways. We traveled, hiked, and went wine tasting. We created new friendships and introduced each other to people we had known before. We began to integrate our four children, three of whom no longer lived full time at home, into our lives. Katie, just finishing her second year of college, and Chris, about to start his senior year of high school, invited Terry to go with us on a trip the kids and I had planned before he and I started dating. We were flying to Mazatlan, Mexico, for a vacation and they told me it only seemed right that he should go. I learned international travel was outside Terry's comfort zone, but well within mine. It was important to me that we have vacations that met both our needs, and I wasn't willing to limit my experiences to places we could reach only by motorcycle or car. I loved hopping on a plane and arriving in a foreign environment only hours later. I appreciated Terry's willingness to go despite any discomfort he felt about all the hassles of airports, taxis, and packing.

This was a flinch for me, a reaction to something in my past. Vacations with Pete, my ex, had been difficult primarily because he wanted everything to be an adrenaline-type experience. I preferred exploring different cultures, trying new things, and sharing some of my interests with the kids. I liked hiking and backpacking, sitting by a lake, reading a book, or telling stories around a campfire. For the last few years of our marriage, I had taken Katie and Chris on vacations with other girlfriends and their kids while Pete met friends for his outdoor adventures. I missed doing activities as a family, introducing our children to some of the experiences we had shared prior to their arrival. The logistics of planning meals, coordinating different interests, and dealing with the chaos that came naturally with siblings was difficult for Pete. He wanted to focus on the activity, and the activity itself had to be intense. Inviting Terry to join the kids and me brought out some of my fears. What would Terry really be like? How would we all get along? I already knew the two of us travelled well together, but what might change with the addition of Katie and Chris?

Arriving in Mexico, we set off for our hotel. We settled into a comfortable routine of body surfing, swimming, and relaxing. Most of the time, the four of us stayed together, and Terry seemed comfortable without having any agenda, letting the day and our mood dictate what we did. One afternoon, Terry and I played golf. Another morning Katie and I had spa treatments while Terry and Chris rented jet skis. We all went SCUBA diving, and when Katie couldn't find a way to get her ears to clear, Terry volunteered to return to the boat and hang out with her.

The four of us took a tour into the mountains above Mazatlan, and I was startled by the familiarity I felt. Just after turning sixteen, my stepsister Karen and I went to Mexico for a three-week adventure without our parents, traveling by commercial bus with

Maria, our live-in housekeeper. We visited her hometown in the hills south of Guadalajara, and spent several days touring Mexico City, visiting ancient ruins and floating gardens. Our final stop was a stay in Acapulco where we watched the famous cliff divers, tried SCUBA diving for the first time, and one day, for fun, rented scooters. The streets of the beach town were in terrible condition and we became really proficient at dodging potholes. I loved the people we met and the feeling of being independent, if only for that short time. I had fun sharing my stories of my earlier trip with Terry and the kids.

I later asked Terry if he had really wanted to go on the tour, and he replied, "I wanted to be with all of you. That was the most important thing to me." I felt my fears surfacing at different times, and I shared them with Terry as they came up. Another of my flinches was feeling responsible for everyone, especially my partner. I kept checking in to see if Terry was having a good time, but I had difficulty trusting his answer. Somehow if he wasn't enjoying himself it was my fault for asking him to come, which I knew logically was not true. He listened carefully to my concerns, and shared his reactions. He valued family connections in a manner similar to mine, and he didn't need to be entertained. He appreciated the time we spent together and the activities we were doing. He didn't need intensity, he needed connection. He wanted to feel included, and he believed each of us contributed to that by voicing what was important to us.

We also had our first serious conflict involving one of the kids. Terry and Chris had a difference in opinion about how Chris, at seventeen, was talking to me, and they had some heated words. Chris became very angry and refused to talk to Terry, and Terry felt strongly that they needed to resolve this between them. I felt pulled to jump into the middle of the discussion, replaying my role in both my family growing up and in my marriage. I was often put in the position of mediator, and my profession as therapist in many ways only reinforced that when everyone turned to me for advice. I had to learn how to step back and sit with my emotions, realizing Terry was treating Chris with respect and honesty and that Chris had to learn how to speak his mind without yelling. I had to support them both in finding their own way of relating, man to man. Terry was willing and able to confront uncomfortable emotions without anger and talk until solutions were found. He continued to surprise me by taking responsibility for his half of any relationship, not deferring to me and my expertise as so many others had done before. It was a welcome relief to let go of having to hold everyone together. While this wasn't their last struggle it set the tone for the way they worked out their relationship. The tensions were ultimately resolved, and the vacation was a success. The four of us had built a first layer in the foundation of what would become our new blended family.

Our relationship was becoming serious, and it was time for all the kids to get to know each other. I had spent time with Aaron and Jessica, and Terry knew Katie and Chris, but if we were going to become a family we needed to know if they would get along with each other. Aaron, the oldest of all the kids, had graduated college the previous May and was now working full time, while Jessica, like Katie, was a junior in college. They liked to snowboard, and with the winter holidays coming up we planned a trip to Sun Peaks in British Columbia. Aaron and Jessica would come for part of the time and head back to Seattle to spend Christmas with their mother, while Katie and Chris would stay with us for the entire trip.

We put them in our Volvo wagon for the drive, hoping time without parents would help them bond, and we followed in Terry's truck. That plan didn't exactly work, since we later found out they spent the seven-hour drive time primarily listening to music and reading, not knowing what to talk about. But after arriving at our condo and unpacking, we asked them when they wanted to celebrate Christmas and open their gifts. "Tonight!" they all shouted in unison, so we sent them off into the small village while we set up the tree and arranged the presents. I'm not sure we could have planned it better. They returned an hour later much more relaxed and talkative, and the sharing of gifts, amid much teasing and playfulness, broke up any lingering awkwardness we all might have been feeling. One of my favorite photos of that night is the four of them decked out in their Burger King crowns, which we had impulsively picked up at a meal stop on our way to the condo.

We hadn't told Aaron and Jessica that Chris was gay, feeling this wasn't a major aspect of who he was but simply a fact, like he's five feet ten inches tall. We assumed it would come out naturally whenever it happened, and while we felt they wouldn't have an issue with it, it was still something that could create tension for all of us if it was even a slight problem. Aaron and Chris, like Katie and Jessica, were sharing a room, and Chris, who brought a change of clothes for every possible occasion, was overwhelming their space with his stuff. One afternoon, while Chris and the girls were out snowboarding, Aaron made the comment that Chris really liked clothes.

"I guess girls really like guys who dress well," he said.

Terry and I looked at each other. Do we say something? After a pause, I nodded to Terry and he replied, "Well, Chris isn't actually into girls."

Without skipping a beat, Aaron answered, "Well, I heard guys like it, too," and we both breathed a sigh of relief.

Our family was expanding, and we continued to find ways to work out the challenges that came with blending everyone together. Like all good families, there were moments of tension, and like most siblings, they occasionally argued between themselves. It was hard when the tension was between the kids because I still didn't trust that they had bonded sufficiently to weather too many arguments, but I resisted the urge to jump in, letting them work it out instead. I believe that while they occasionally drove each other crazy, the experiences also helped them become closer.

We now knew everyone could get along, and while Terry and I seemed to have an intuitive sense that our relationship was solid and that we planned to stay together, the topic of marriage hadn't come up. Neither of us seemed to have any feeling of urgency. So I was quite surprised when one morning Terry showed me a flyer for closet systems and seemed very interested in my opinions.

"What do you think I should put in the master closet?" he asked.

I looked at him blankly. "Whatever you think you might need. What do you want to put in there?"

"Well, you never know. I may need to make space for someone else's things and I'd want to make sure it would be what they would want as well," he replied.

It took a few minutes for his words to register. "Um, excuse me? I think we need to talk."

We had our second "sitting on the curb" conversation, this time on the couch in Terry's living room. It was a serious discussion about our future. We both had found the right person. We had, in less than a year, created a relationship that we could see lasting the rest of our lives. We talked about our fears, each of us coming from recent divorces. We still had flinches when we reacted from past experiences and had to remember that this relationship was different. Terry realized during this discussion that there was an issue he still needed to work through, and I encouraged him to talk with the therapist he had met with previously. I didn't want to be in the position of becoming his counselor, and I wanted him to have the freedom to speak about anything without any hint of pressure from me. I was both comfortable there weren't any secrets that would come up, and scared that there might be something even he wasn't aware of. After a single visit, he understood what had been bothering him, and it was a lingering fear based on his previous marriage. Once he understood what he was feeling, he was ready to move forward. While it had been hard for me to sit quietly, I was glad I had stayed out of his way and let him figure things out for himself.

Shortly after these discussions Terry proposed. This time I said yes without any hesitation. We barely had time to use the shelves he put into his condominium. Instead, we bought a new home and designed the closets together.

CHAPTER SEVEN

Bun Burner

Terry was invited to join some friends for a day ride from Seattle to Hurricane Ridge, a national park that was a ferry crossing away on the Olympic Peninsula. I always noticed large groups of motorcyclists riding together and wondered what it might be like to ride with them. When someone unfamiliar with motorcycling thinks about bikes, Harley-Davidson often comes to mind. Most casual, suburban riders ride them, or similar cruiser models, preferring the image of the iconic bike. This was such a group, and they were very friendly and welcoming as we met them at the dock for the ferry that would take us on the short trip across Puget Sound to the peninsula. I learned one of the perks of motorcycling—we were able to cut to the front of the long ferry line and get on the boat first. We stood by our bikes, watching the crossing at almost eye level with the sea. As we exited, we formed a group of perhaps twenty bikes, and headed down the two-lane road towards Port Angeles and the turn for the Ridge.

Unlike long-distance riders, this group stopped frequently for food, for gas, for cigarettes, for anything. We were going so slowly I was starting to get bored and fidgety. When we finally entered the park gate, and were about to ascend the long, twisty mountain road, Terry pulled to the side to let the other bikes get a decent head start. For once we had a clear road ahead of us and could enjoy riding at a normal speed for at least a few minutes. In far too short a time we caught up with the group and had to slow down and ride in formation. At any available opportunity Terry would slow down, let them get ahead, and then catch up to them in no time at all. I realized two important things on this ride. One, I really don't like riding in large groups and having to conform to someone else's schedule and agenda, and two, riding at such a slow pace is torture to me—I actually like going fast. I was glad I had the opportunity to figure this out on my own.

Just before moving into our new house Terry went to Las Vegas to spend a weekend at a riding school run by former Grand Prix motorcycle world champion Freddie Spencer. It was held on racetrack, with students riding a fleet of sportbikes. Terry's goal was to improve his cornering skills. He called me after the first day, exhausted and frustrated, not sure he could adapt to the new ways they were teaching him. When he arrived home after the second day with a videotape of himself on the track, he could barely walk but he was elated. His body had figured out how to move smoothly through tight corners at high speeds. The next test was to see how his new knowledge transferred to the RT.

Unlike the techniques he'd been taught in trainings he attended before, at Freddie's he learned to put his weight on the inside footpeg, which forced him to push the bike more upright to balance it. In addition, he was shown how to apply the brake going into the curve so he wasn't afraid to use it in corners. I experienced an immediate difference when we went out for a ride. The bike barely leaned over no matter how sharp the curve or how fast the corner. Terry slid off the seat, and as he pushed the bike, it stayed upright. I loved it! We could now go on twisty roads at a nice clip, and I was more comfortable and relaxed. Terry was amused when other riders saw him hanging off the side of the bike as if he were on the track.

Our wedding was planned for May 21st, six weeks after the move into our new home. Coincidentally, the Iron Butt Association announced a National Meet, a mini-conference for the long-distance community, in Omaha, Nebraska, the second weekend in May. As luck and calendars would have it, this was one week before our wedding. We both wanted to attend the National, and I jokingly told Terry I always wanted to go to Omaha and I wouldn't marry him unless he took me there first.

To make the trip more interesting we planned to ride a Bun Burner Gold from Seattle to Omaha. A BBG is 1500 miles in less than twenty-four hours, certainly doable for us and a fun challenge. Our itinerary was to ride the first hundred and fifty miles from our home in Snoqualmie and spend the night. From there it was 1540 miles to Omaha, perfect for finishing the BBG at the Meet without having any extra miles to ride at the end when we were exhausted. Unwilling to risk another stay at our favorite hourly motel in Moses Lake, Washington, we made reservations at one of the decent hotels along the freeway, and started from there early the next morning.

As we neared Spokane, we'd ridden less than a hundred miles and were getting a good rhythm going when we encountered road construction. Forced to follow a pilot car and a truck spraying oil on the highway going barely twenty miles per hour, Terry's frustration was palpable. I tried to stay upbeat, wanting to help him feel better so his irritation wouldn't take a toll on him later. He said our average pace determined our success or failure, and that every minute we were stuck in slow traffic was a minute we couldn't afford. We had to be even more diligent on a BBG than on a SaddleSore if we were to complete the miles in time. It would be too hard to make it up later in the day when the effects of being tired would be greater and we would inevitably get slower every time we stopped for necessities such as gas or food. Just as on a SaddleSore, speeding would wear Terry out, so maximizing efficiency was the key to the ride. Being stuck in traffic was not helping.

We also failed to consider the weather. Although it was well into May, Mother Nature hadn't finished with winter. When she decided to unleash a flurry of blizzards in South Dakota we had already completed our first 1000 miles despite the morning's delay, and were still on a good pace for the BBG. I was getting cold, but I was unwilling to quit. As pillion, I don't get the wind protection Terry does. Motorcycles are designed to create a "bubble" that forces the air above or around the rider, but the bubble doesn't completely protect the passenger. As a result I need more gear to stay warm, something neither of us yet understood. My arms were chilled, and the backs of my legs were getting blasted with the cold air. I didn't tell Terry how I was feeling or that I might be starting to have problems. I'm not sure whether I didn't want to worry him or didn't want to admit to myself I was struggling. It was dark outside and I couldn't tell where we were, but I kept thinking we'd descend out of the mountains any minute, the air would warm up, and we'd be fine. But when the snow began sticking to the roads, especially on the overpasses, we started to worry about our safety. With the wind blowing harder and harder, and the flakes coming right at his face, Terry said his vision felt like the images of warp speed on the old TV series *Star Trek*. He was struggling to see and to keep the bike on the road.

Reluctantly, we admitted we needed to get off the highway. Slowing down to almost a crawl until we could find an off-ramp with services, we finally spotted a hotel and checked in. As I undressed, I couldn't stop shivering. No matter what I did, I couldn't get warm. We piled on blankets and huddled together for over a half an hour until my body temperature finally returned to normal. I didn't realize I had become mildly hypothermic. Another lesson learned—let Terry know when I'm uncomfortable, and be willing to stop. We decided I needed to buy better electrically heated clothing, similar to an electric blanket with wires running throughout and a plug that connects to the power on the bike. I had been wearing only a Gerbing heated jacket, but the company also made pants, socks, and gloves, which I put on my list to buy as soon as we got back to Seattle.

We arrived in Omaha having completed a Bun Burner, 1500 miles in 36 hours, rather than the Bun Burner Gold. While it was quite an accomplishment considering the conditions, I was somewhat frustrated that we hadn't completed our BBG. I thought about what we might have done differently but the reality was we couldn't control the weather. Part of the challenge of long-distance riding was overcoming difficulties, but another was recognizing when to stop and try again another time. I also realized I didn't enjoy the SaddleSore challenges as much as I enjoyed rallies. On mileage rides such as the SaddleSore or the BBG, there wasn't much for me to do. Interstates are usually monotonous and boring, and while I enjoyed sightseeing, I wanted to be more of a partner and not just a passenger. Rallies kept me more engaged and helped Terry and me feel more connected. Certified rides might be fun from time to time but they weren't going to be a high priority for us.

Our immediate priority upon our return home was our wedding, held the following weekend. It was blessed by both our ministers, with our son Aaron, his girlfriend Robyn, our daughter Jessica, her boyfriend Alex, our daughter Katie and our son Chris as our witnesses. We followed the early-morning ceremony with a lively open house in the afternoon, surrounded by friends and family. We had officially blended our separate worlds into one.

CHAPTER EIGHT

Competition

It was shaping up to be a busy year, both on and off the bike. We had moved, completed a Bun Burner certified ride, and gotten married. We were still planning to take a leisurely ride to Ohio in early August, and fly to Ireland with our daughter Katie and part of her college equestrian team at the end of summer. So the only rally we signed up for in 2005 was the Utah 1088, and this time I had a better idea of what to expect. At the riders' meeting Friday night, Steve announced the first bonus, a "slow ride." To score the points the rider had to take at least a minute to ride the distance between two pieces of tape about fifty feet apart in the parking lot without putting a foot down. After the meeting, one of the top riders tried it and didn't even come close. Seeing that, most of the others weren't even going to try. It was really hard for me to give up on something without trying it, but we believed it would be too hard for a two-up team. None of the few brave souls who attempted it that year were successful.

We were introduced to a new element in our riding—head-to-head competition. As we sat in the parking lot at the riders' meeting we heard "We're going to kick your ass!" and "Bring it on!" coming from somewhere near us. Another couple, Tammy and Monte Leveaux, riding two-up in their first rally, was challenging us to a duel. These words were foreign to our concept of rallying. I could feel the pressure inside me building. I'm a competitive person, but I dislike competing against other people when I'm uncomfortable with my own skills. I hate the idea of looking foolish, being judged, or failing publicly. Going all out, doing my best, and being soundly beaten is a different story. Competing against ourselves was much more comfortable than feeling pressure to outperform someone else, and here we were suddenly engaging in trash talk with a couple we had just met. This internal pressure usually spurs me to try harder to prove myself. My thinking clouds, I rush through decisions, and I become easily irritated. Terry didn't know this about me yet.

Following the riders' meeting Saturday morning, we headed to our room to plan our route. I wanted to race through things and get on the road, but Terry kept slowing me down. I got annoyed with his methodical approach since it was obvious to me what we should do. He forced me to go bonus by bonus, marking the main route while I read off the point values. He was patient with me and I tried to be patient with him. Using our paper map, we finally had each bonus in place, and each checkpoint was circled with the time it would be open. There were a few GPS-only bonuses, which meant we had to find them by their latitude and longitude, and figure out where they were on the map.

*****BONUS NUMBER X IS WORTH 4114 POINTS (4114) THIS IS ANOTHER OF THE SEEK AND FIND GPS QUESTIONS, AND LIKE BEFORE, IT'S LISTED EARLY IN THE PAPERWORK BECAUSE OF THE POINT VALUE. IT SHOULD ALSO BE NOTED THAT

THIS BONUS IS NOT LISTED IN THE ORDER OF OCCURANCE. THIS IS A TWO PART BONUS, AND BOTH PARTS MUST BE COMPLETED IN ORDER TO RECEIVE THE POINTS. FIRST, FIND THE LOCATION OF THE FOLLOWING GPS COORDINATES **N 41° 14. 214' AND W 105° 26. 178'**. SECOND, TAKE A POLAROID PICTURE OF A STATUE LOCATED WITHIN 20 FEET OF THE COORDINATES. THIS BONUS IS AVAILABLE TO ALL RIDERS, AND IS AVAILABLE AT ANY TIME DURING THE RALLY.

PICTURE _____ ODOMETER _____ TIME _____

With the markings done, we were finally ready to devise our strategy. Our plan was to have places we could cut out bonuses if we had problems, and choice points we could use to make major route adjustments. We picked a route that deviated from the main route, blowing off one bonus that required a detour of about forty miles out of the way, but which gave us plenty of time to get a far more valuable GPS bonus. Steve's route sent us on a long, twisty two-lane road early in the rally but there were no bonus points that way. By sticking to the interstate, Terry would be more rested later in the evening. He wanted to skip the Delicate Arch bonus later in the rally because he thought it would take too much time and effort. It had a high point value and I didn't want to give it up, especially since I wanted to beat the other couples. To get the bonus we'd have to ride fifteen miles of slow, tourist-filled road inside Arches National Park, and then hike a mile and a half uphill to the bonus itself. I humored him, figuring I could talk him into it later.

This was our first rally using a backpack instead of a tank bag. Most riders have some type of bag on the gas tank in which they put snacks, flashlights, rally packs, and other small items. Terry had one when we first met, but it was distracting for him to be fishing in it for things while riding, and with me on the back it made sense to move our supplies to a place where I could easily reach them. We fit the rally pack, camera, snacks, and even spare gloves for me into different compartments, and while Terry wore the pack, it rested on the seat between us and didn't put any strain on him. We put several peanut-butter-and-jelly sandwiches in the trunk on the back of the bike to minimize food stops. We could snack whenever we stopped for a bonus photo or gas. I was slowly changing my ideas of what was necessary and what was luxury. Stopping to sit at fast-food restaurants had become a luxury.

Terry's confidence hadn't been rattled by the competition, nor did he feel any pressure to respond to it. He kept asking, "What's our plan, what can we do, what sounds fun and interesting to us?" He encouraged me when I got too hot during the day and too cold at night. He reminded me we were riding for ourselves and no one else. We'd had no expectations on the first 1088, and here we were on only our second rally and I was expecting us to be great. Logically, I knew it was enough that we had returned to Utah, we had gotten married, and we were continuing to build an amazing relationship. But inside, I wanted to beat Tammy and Monte!

Early in the first leg we hit road construction on Route 150 on our way to take a photo of a sign in front of a nudist colony. Terry rode up the shoulder of the road past the vehicles stopped in front of us to get ahead of them when the flagger turned his sign around. I was torn between wanting to get ahead and being a rule follower. My siblings nicknamed me Lily White as a teenager, the goodie-goodie. It still surprises me when Lily shows up, like now when I was afraid the other drivers or the flagger would get angry and we'd get in trouble. In situations like this Terry is a rule bender, often seeing rules as suggestions and not worrying about getting caught. Neither of us knew if there actually was a rule about passing the stopped cars—I just didn't want to be yelled at. Luckily, as we reached the flagger he switched the STOP sign around to SLOW and, smiling, waved us on. We learned later that Tammy and Monte got stuck at this same backup for twenty minutes, which contributed to them missing the first checkpoint. Our decision to skip the earlier bonus and avoid the twisty road, and Terry's rule bending, paid off.

A while later, riding east on I-70 and the turn for Moab, the location of the next checkpoint, we were joined by our friend Jim Owen, who was taking the same exit off the interstate. As both bikes reached the bottom of the off-ramp we stopped to chat with him about some minor confusion in the rally packet. Jim asked if we were going to the Delicate Arch, and Terry said no. Jim mentioned that we were at least an hour ahead of schedule, that the Arch was worth a lot of points, and we'd be riding right past the park on our way to Moab. I really wanted to go, and told Terry we should. He agreed to follow Jim to the parking lot and said we'd make a decision there. I knew once we were there I'd be able to talk him into it.

The instructions said you had to hike to the Arch, and it had to be visible in the photo. We all interpreted this to mean the parking-lot viewpoint wasn't acceptable, that the Arch was too far away to be captured on film, and the word hike meant just that. I volunteered to walk the one-and-a-half miles while Terry rested by the bike and watched Jim's and my gear. Stripping to bike shorts, a T-shirt, and motorcycling boots, I grabbed the backpack, camera, and water bottle. Just before we took off, Terry added a spare pack of film to the backpack.

Jim and I started up the trail at a very brisk pace. I was in good shape, but within a very short time I was barely able to breathe. Jim, a commercial airline pilot, said he had been flying to Geneva, Switzerland, and on his layovers went hiking in the Alps. Terry and I live at 800 feet above sea level, and Arches is at about 5000 feet. The elevation was killing me but at least I had a reason for feeling so out of shape. I told Jim to go on ahead while I kept hiking at a steady pace. I was surprised by the number of tourists who paid no attention to any of the motorcyclists in full gear scampering up and down the rocky trail, certainly an oddity in most national parks I've visited. I noticed a temporarily abandoned Aerostich suit tossed to the side of the trail—apparently the rider had succumbed to the heat and decided to strip midway up the mountain. I doubted it was in any danger of being stolen in such a strange location, but I did wonder what he would do if he came back to find it gone.

Thrilled to finally reach the top, I crawled over to the opening in the rocks to take my picture of the Arch. The wind was blowing furiously and as I pushed the button to take the photo nothing happened—the camera was out of film. I had a moment of panic until I remembered Terry's foresight in sending a spare pack. I changed the cartridge and took the picture. Then I shoved everything back in the pack and practically ran the mile-and-a-half back down the mountain. I was gasping for breath when I reached the parking lot and the bike. Terry asked what I thought of the Arch. I realized I had no idea what it looked like. I hadn't taken the time to actually see it.

Late in the afternoon, after riding through a heavy rain without my extra layers of clothing, I got really cold. I was getting a headache and generally feeling miserable. I couldn't tell if I was dealing with allergies or a lack of caffeine. We stopped at a gas station to pump me full of allergy pills and wash them down with a Dr. Pepper. I struggled with adding the clothing I needed to get warm again—every movement was slow and uncomfortable. I knew Terry wanted to keep going, and that he was frustrated by my addiction to caffeine, but he remained supportive. He fought the urge to make me move faster, giving me the time and space to add layers while encouraging me to drink fluids. Terry, like many long-distance riders, gave up caffeine because it impaired his ability to fend off tiredness and caused spikes in energy that fell off to deeper exhaustion. He had encouraged me to quit as well, but my love of chai tea lattes was too strong.

Not long after we stopped, another couple from the rally, Steve and Julie, pulled in for gas. They looked well rested, and we discovered they had covered more miles than we had. When they left Terry said he thought they were probably ahead of us in points. This added to my frustration at our long stop. I blamed myself for not putting on warmer gear before I got cold and for not recognizing my need for caffeine. I felt discouraged, but I knew we had to keep pushing on, no matter our final standing.

A while later, we stopped again for gas and reevaluated our plan. The main route was going to put us on slow, two-lane roads. We'd be shooting photos in the dark, which with the primitive technology of Polaroids was hard to do. We would have to use our bike's headlights, auxiliary lights, and any flashlights we might be carrying to illuminate whatever we had to photograph, and the time that took was time we weren't riding. Terry checked the GPS to determine our current mileage, and realized that because of the changes we had made in the beginning, avoiding the twisty road, we would now be coming up short on miles if we stuck with the main route. We debated riding west toward Ely, Nevada, where we could pick up a few bonuses while we piled on miles, but by our best calculation we would arrive in Salt Lake City an hour late and be classified DNF (did not finish). We agreed to head east on I-70 riding at the higher freeway speeds for an hour or so before turning around and getting back on the main route for the last leg. We picked up a bonus in Green River we would normally have skipped because it was only available after midnight and in a direction no one should really be going at that time of the Rally, but our plan was no longer about getting points. I was now resigned to the hope we would still be finishers.

Once we were moving again my mood lifted. The ride east went quickly, and as we turned around and headed back toward the west, we were treated to an amazing storm off in the distance. The beauty of the early evening sky was punctuated by ominous black clouds and flashes of lightning, and it was hypnotizing to watch. Slowly we realized the storm was getting closer. I asked Terry if he'd ever ridden in weather like this, and what we should do if we were caught in it. Rain was one thing, but lightning was another. After all, we were the tallest object around as far as we could see. Before he could answer, we were hit with a blast of water as lightning flashed all around us. We saw an overpass and pulled underneath it to get some protection. Then Terry said, "Hey, we're the world's toughest motorcycle riders—why are we scared of some measly rain?" and pulled back out into the downpour. I heard the thunder as it roared by, but the storm passed as quickly as it had come, and we were once again in the quiet and solitude of the night.

Arriving at the checkpoint, we saw a few other riders. Most quickly stopped in long enough to prove they were there, got gas, and took off again, but Terry was tired and didn't want to get back on the bike without resting. He found a quiet spot on the concrete slab behind the station and grabbed a quick nap. I sat down and reread the rally packet to make sure I understood each bonus, and had a snack. Our plan had worked, and our mileage was where we needed it to be for the final leg. We could now resume our original route, picking up more bonuses as we slowly made our way back to the hotel.

Sometime just before dawn, I found myself struggling for the first time to stay awake. I was having micro naps, dozing for a second then jerking awake suddenly. Terry felt my movements, and asked if I was OK. The back seats of touring bikes are very comfortable, and it's not uncommon for passengers to fall asleep, sometimes for long stretches. I talked to myself, looked up at the stars, and did everything to shake off exhaustion. I preferred staying awake and being part of the action, but I was struggling. The sun, thankfully, soon came up, and with it my energy, and I was fine for the rest of the rally.

At the finishers' banquet, I dreaded hearing the final standings. With our struggles, I assumed we had done poorly. But as Steve first called up the third-place couple, then Tammy and Monte, I realized we had placed first in the two-up category. It was extremely satisfying, and I wanted to be smug and harass Tammy after her display the previous morning, but I resisted the urge because I knew how close we had come to blowing it ourselves. We learned some of their decisions in the first leg caused them to miss the first checkpoint, and some of ours, such as skipping a bonus and jumping the line in the construction, helped us. Catching our mileage shortage in time to correct it also made a huge difference. They now understood how challenging a rally could be and had more respect for the sport, and we had respect for the ride they had completed. They vowed to return the following year and we knew they, and all the others we rode against, would push us to keep improving.

Riding home from Utah, we talked a lot about competition, rallying, and what we thought about it. The twenty-six-hour rally was a lot of fun. I liked both the camaraderie of the other riders and the times we were alone, just us and the bike. I loved riding down odd side roads and seeing things we might otherwise never see. I appreciated the solitude in the middle of the night, looking up at the sky full of stars with no one around for miles. I was intrigued by the puzzle of trying to decide which route to take, and how to adjust when plans suddenly changed. I didn't like the stress of planning on the clock, and I was often uncomfortable with the feelings I had about winning or losing. Overall, I saw these competitions as opportunities to push myself emotionally, physically, and mentally.

I also spent time reflecting on why I didn't want to ride my own bike. After our first 1088, when I met two women, Coni Fitch and Maura Gatensby, who each rode solo, I remember thinking to myself, "Why *aren't* I riding by myself? I *should* be riding my own bike." I felt an internal pressure to learn to ride, so when we came home from Utah I signed up for the local Motorcycle Safety Foundation class. I learned how to ride on a little Honda 250 in a huge parking lot, and was surprised by how much I remembered from my brief experience at fifteen. I passed the licensing test easily, bought my own motorcycle, and went out for some short rides both with and without Terry. When I rode alone I had a grand time, and enjoyed being in the rider's seat. I even liked the "coolness factor" of riding solo.

But I kept coming back to the question, "Why do I continue to ride as a pillion?" I realized my reasons went back to the start of my relationship with Terry. I came from a background that highly valued independence. I backpacked across the Sierras many times, always carrying my own gear. I'd lived alone, travelled alone, and felt capable and competent making decisions on my own. Riding my own motorcycle would seem to be natural for me, and part of it was. And yet, there was something special about riding together, on the same bike, that appealed to me. My first marriage had too much separateness. I wanted to be in a relationship where sharing the entire experience together was a priority, focused not on independence but on interdependence.

I loved being with Terry and sharing the unique experiences we had as a two-up team. When we were competing, I liked working together to achieve a common goal. I helped pull him through some tough times, and he encouraged me when I was down. We strategized and discussed every detail and decision we had to face. I frustrated him at times with my inconsistencies, and he frustrated me at times with his stubbornness, but we were sharing our frustrations and building our history together. I loved knowing we were competing together, not against each other. We shared completely in the victories, and picked each other up when we lost focus. The struggles to interweave our lives were compounded on a single motorcycle, where we had so little space and were constantly connected. How we navigated our rides was becoming synonymous with how we navigated our marriage.

CHAPTER NINE

Changes

We had never taken a long-distance ride simply for pleasure. Until now, all our trips had focused on endurance. When we saw that the 2005 BMW Motorcycle Owners of America rally would be held in Lima, Ohio, just a few miles south of Terry's hometown, we decided this was perfect timing for our wedding reception with his family and a vacation ride for us. Terry came up with the idea of riding across Highway 2, which paralleled the northern border of the U.S., as far east as Duluth, Minnesota, then riding around the northern shore of Lake Superior, and finally turning south through Michigan and into Ohio. We had about 2800 miles to cover and five days to do it. For us, that meant no clocks to watch or high miles to accumulate. We needed to average just over five hundred miles a day, and we planned stops at sights we each wanted to visit.

We started our trip by joining Highway 2 just outside Wenatchee, where it paralleled the eastern edge of the Columbia River for several miles before climbing out of the canyons and into farmlands. This was a section of road I had never been on, having always driven on the other side of the river, and it was fun to have a new perspective. It was so peaceful avoiding the interstate as we rode through the endless miles of wheat fields, stopping to eat in tiny diners along the two-lane highway. We spent one night in Kalispell, Montana, in a beautifully restored historic hotel in the older part of town. I had never been to Glacier, and while the cloudy weather didn't cooperate, it occasionally lifted enough to give us some glimpses of the beauty of the Going to the Sun Road. Descending into the flatlands of eastern Montana and North Dakota, our route took us through rural farmlands that reminded me of being a kid, driving through small towns with no chain restaurants in sight. Terry was excited to stop in Rugby, North Dakota, the geographical center of North America, and we took our picture sitting in front of the obelisk marking the spot. My only complaint was the quality of many of the roads. Years of neglect made for rough, bumpy and uneven surfaces, jarring the bike as we made our way east.

Our protective outer clothing was made by a company called Aerostich/RiderWearHouse, and their factory and store were in an old industrial part of Duluth, in an ancient brick building that gave no hint of the activity inside. Before we left home Terry arranged for a personal tour of the facility. We watched as they explained the precision that goes into every suit made individually by one of the people sitting in front of us. The pride of the workers was evident, and seeing the attention to detail and safety took some of the sting out of the price we had paid for our gear.

I was disappointed in the ride around Lake Superior, thinking it would be a stunningly beautiful ride, but it wasn't as lovely as I had anticipated. Whenever we turned away from the lake it was mostly kilometer after kilometer of roads passing through trees on either side of us, and even the lakeshore itself wasn't as dramatic as I had envisioned. We had heard the Mackinac

Bridge, a steel-grate span between Lakes Michigan and Huron, could be intimidating for motorcyclists, especially navigating the grating in the wind or rain, but as we approached Terry realized the outer lane was fully paved and no problem for the motorcycle. Soon I was watching the lake off to our sides and the water rushing below.

Kevin and Lisa, our friends from Seattle, were at the MOA rally, and we spent a day with them at the fairgrounds people-watching and checking out the bikes and gear. Most of our time was spent with Terry's family, sharing the joy of our recent marriage and seeing relatives with whom we didn't often get a chance to speak. Jessica, Katie, Aaron, and Robyn flew in for the reception, while Chris was unable to attend due to prior work commitments. Terry's mother, who had suffered a brain aneurism the previous October, was able to join us for most of the day. It was one of the last times she was able to leave the nursing home prior to her death the following December. Being with her, watching her joy as she spent time surrounded by family, was a highlight of our trip.

We planned a SaddleSore 2000 on the way home to once again make a boring ride more interesting. It was essentially back-to-back SaddleSores, 2000 miles in 48 hours. The route took us on the interstate through Illinois, Wisconsin, Minnesota, North Dakota, Montana, and Idaho, and finally home. We expected Chicago to be the hardest part of the ride because of the heavy traffic and confusing freeways, but it turned out to be western Wisconsin where we were caught in torrential rains, wind, and lightning. Terry could see the road only by slowly and carefully following the taillights of trucks ahead of us. We debated getting off the highway but there really weren't any safe places to stop. It was both scary and exhilarating to watch the lightning crackling all around us. I wondered if we were stupid for pushing on. I hated riding in this kind of weather, but we reasoned we'd be better off continuing west since the storm was quickly pushing east. After what felt like days but was really only hours, the rain let up and we pulled into a gas station to swap our wet gear for the few dry things we had, grab a quick snack, and pump some gas. Being on the clock meant we didn't want to stop any longer than we absolutely needed to, and we got right back on the road. We were committed to finishing the SaddleSore, and the rain had slowed our pace considerably.

Riding east had been a lovely and relaxing trip, even on the many stretches of Highway 2 that were so poorly maintained. But it was clear the road had taken a toll on my body and it was becoming difficult to sit on the bike for long periods. Despite riding on smoother interstates as we traveled west, my tailbone ached as the miles piled up. I didn't want to quit, but I didn't want to keep riding, either. The pain was becoming increasingly unbearable—it hurt to sit and it hurt to stand up. We still had to ride home whether we did it as a SaddleSore or not, but I wasn't sure I cared any longer about the IBA certification. Terry, who had completed numerous IBA rides and didn't need another one to feel any more accomplished, wisely left the decision to stop or go up to me.

I still regretted not finishing the Bun Burner Gold on our way to Omaha, and I didn't want another failed ride, especially because of my body. My competitiveness kicked in and I opted to grit my teeth and tough it out. I had a brief respite when we stopped for a few hours sleep in Missoula, Montana. We hit the 2000-mile mark in Ritzville, Washington, well within the forty-eight-hour time frame. I was pleased I chose to keep riding, but there wasn't time for much celebrating since my tailbone and I still had almost 200 miles to go before we could actually get off the bike.

It was becoming obvious the RT wasn't working for me over long distances. I was limited to a few thousand miles before pain interfered with my enjoyment of the ride, and my discomfort on this last trip forced us to seriously confront the issue. While we loved the feel of the RT, the ergonomics were killing me, and Terry's other bike, the GS Adventure, wasn't any better. If we were going to continue riding endurance events, we needed a bike that fit us both.

There are only a few models of touring bikes that work well for couples. The two we seriously considered were the BMW LT, and the Gold Wing by Honda. Both are large, comfortable motorcycles with reasonable amounts of storage. Since my seat was the crucial decider, we needed to test-ride both bikes. A touring company near us rented Hondas, and we spent a day taking a short ride, just a few hundred miles, around Mount Rainier. Stopping at a red light in Enumclaw, another couple on a Gold Wing signaled to us they wanted to tell us something.

"One of your headlamps is out," the man said as he lifted his visor to speak.

"Thanks, we know," Terry replied.

"*Please* tell me we don't look that old!" was all I could say to Terry as the very nice man rode off.

We both hated the idea of a Gold Wing. No matter how many excellent long-distance riders had one, it still had a reputation as an old person's bike. Its derogatory nickname was "the Barcalounger." It didn't have the sportier reputation of the BMWs. We just didn't believe we had enough gray hairs to own one.

Still, even with terribly worn-out stock shock absorbers, which caused severe jarring every time we hit a bump, I could tell the difference. My seating position was much more comfortable and I could see the advantages of the added storage space for long-distance rides. Terry was surprised by the engine's power when he passed a car. The Wing didn't handle as crisply as our BMW but Terry believed he could easily adjust to the changes.

We test-rode the LT, crossing our fingers it would be the right solution for us, but within fifty miles we knew it wasn't. The ergonomics were the same as the RT, putting too much pressure on my tailbone, and it would ultimately cause the problems that were making us switch bikes in the first place. I struggled with the decision, knowing how much we both loved the RT, and I felt guilty asking Terry to give it up just for me. He reminded me that I mattered more to him than a brand of motorcycle, and that it was more important that we have a bike we both enjoyed riding so we could be together. When we factored in repair and reliability issues, we agreed the ease of finding dealers who could work on the Honda was a definite plus, and our decision was made.

We knew the model, color, and options we wanted, and were prepared to buy one and ride it off the showroom floor. The new 2006 Wings would have significant changes, making the

2005s less desirable. We asked the salesperson at a highly recommended dealer if there were any discounts on the older model. She only offered a small discount on accessories such as clothing, which we didn't need. The actual bike we wanted, a gray 2005 GL1800 with ABS, wasn't in their showroom, and they'd have to swap for one with another dealer. She wasn't willing to budge. Walking outside, Terry called another local dealer, and asked the salesman if they had the model we were looking for.

"Hold on, let me check," he said, putting the phone down to survey their inventory.

"Yes," he replied, coming back on the line.

"We'll be right over."

The young guy who had spoken with us was eager to sell us the bike, and practically fell out of his chair when we told him we wanted to buy it on the spot. We had done our homework and offered him a reasonable price. He ran to his manager, and returned minutes later, out of breath, to say yes, they'd accept our offer. We finalized the paperwork and were now the proud owners of a shiny new Honda.

The following winter was devoted to working on the Wing. We carried heated gear, a radar detector, auxiliary lighting, and a GPS unit, all of which had to be attached to the bike and wired to power. Terry worked with a local motorcyclist and welder, Bill McAvan, to design, build, and install a tail-dragger auxiliary gas tank that would increase our fuel capacity and extend our range to almost 350 miles between fill-ups. A tail-dragger sits behind the rear wheel on the back of the bike so that there is still a seat for the pillion. Terry asked my opinion on different decisions he had to make, wanting me to be a part of the process, but I wasn't interested in watching him take the bike apart and put it back together. I preferred planning trips, inviting friends over for dinner, and offering my encouragement for all his hard work. Together, I think we kept a good balance of work and play. Terry attended to the details while I made sure we took breaks and had other experiences to round out our relationship.

CHAPTER TEN

What Have We Done Now?

Making the decision to sign up for the 2006 Utah 1088 was easy. It would be our third time, and we both looked forward to seeing the people we had become friends with as well as riding the rally. Deciding to enter the lottery for the 2007 Iron Butt Rally was much harder. Riding in the IBR had been a fantasy of Terry's since he first heard George Barnes speak at the BMW-MOA Rally in 2001. It had never occurred to me to put it on my bucket list.

The Iron Butt Rally lasts 11 days, and riders often travel nearly 11,000 miles in that time. It takes place every two years and is usually held in late August. Like in the Utah 1088, entrants earn points by riding to various bonus locations. Unlike the 1088, those locations can be anywhere in the U.S. or Canada, and the list of potential bonuses is greater. No consideration is given for bad weather, and riders have been known to ride through rain, sleet, snow, severe thunderstorms, hurricanes and the occasional tornado. Unlike the 1088, the IBR has no required mileage. Instead a rider must earn a minimum number of bonus points during the rally to be considered a finisher. Additional achievement levels—gold, silver, and bronze—can be reached by earning more than the minimum required points. First-time finishers earn a three-digit membership number to replace their previously assigned number. Currently the IBA membership is well over 50,000, so the prestige of a three-digit number is well worth the agony of competing in the Rally—in fact, it's essentially the only reward for finishers. As of 2005, only 326 people had officially finished the Iron Butt Rally, fewer than the number of people who have been into space, and of that number there were only five couples, each of whom earned their own low IBA number.

Terry talked frequently about riding in the IBR, and while I didn't want to spoil his fantasy it was hard for me to imagine anything more than the twenty-six-hour rallies we had already done. We had reached a point, however, where neither of us could visualize Terry competing solo, which meant whatever we did, we'd do it as a team. Entrants to the rally are picked primarily by lottery, with special considerations given to previous finishers, riders on unique motorcycles such as older classics or bikes with very small engines, or other factors the rally organizers found intriguing. Each category had its own lottery, and it wasn't uncommon for those special groups to take up a third or more of the one hundred spots available. The remaining places were filled with first-time IBR riders, and the odds of being chosen out of the hundreds who applied were slim.

I took some refuge in the notion that so few people were ever picked in the lottery that I could indulge Terry and we could apply. He'd entered the drawing once before, in 2005, and hadn't been chosen, so I felt reasonably confident I could appear to be very supportive while trusting this was, in reality, an exercise in futility. Win-win for me, with the added bonus that I could be sympathetic and kind when our names weren't drawn.

Terry filled out the entry forms online with as much information as he could. There were standard questions about experience, type of motorcycle, and age. He asked me what to put for my profession, and rather than writing out "Licensed Marriage and Family Therapist" I suggested "psychotherapist," a shorthand we often use to differentiate us from physical and occupational therapists. One question asked something like, "Is there anything else unique about you you'd like to add?" We answered jokingly, "Lynda's a therapist so if we get stressed we can pull to the side of the road and talk about our feelings." After completing the form, Terry printed it so I could proofread it.

"*Psycho therapist* is not two words," I pointed out.

With that correction, some more laughing, and not a little bit of anxiety, Terry hit the "submit" button and we proceeded to wait. The application deadline was in March, and the drawing would be held sometime in June. I was surprised by my building anxiety as the date approached. I had very little knowledge of it other than following our friend Jim Owen in '05, who had been leading for the first two legs when his bike broke down 700 miles from the finish. While I had no idea why I'd want to ride in the Rally, by now I also hated the idea of not getting in. The acceptance/rejection email would be sent from Lisa Landry—the 2007 Iron Butt Rally Master—to Terry, and all I could do was wait as patiently as possible for him to let me know the results. My emails and calls increased in frequency as the deadline neared.

"Well?"

"No news yet."

That was our primary conversation for quite a few days, until finally, a long pause, and:

"We got an email from Lisa."

"And?"

"I waited till I had you on the phone to open it," he answered.

"*Well, then open it NOW!*" I yelled.

"Congratulations..." it began.

"Oh my God, we got in!" we both cried simultaneously, our voices a mixture of disbelief, exhilaration, and terror. I tried to listen but my mind was already racing as he finished reading the email that ended with, "Welcome aboard and so the insanity begins!"

What in the world had we done, and how in the world could we do this? I didn't know whether to laugh or to cry, so I went into denial, overwhelmed by the pressure I suddenly felt and oblivious to what lay ahead. "We'll be fine, no big deal, we can do this and still live our normal lives," I thought as I tried to remain calm. Terry was both ecstatic and anxious, and handled it by going into over-functioning mode, immediately making lists and figuring out what we would need to do over the next year to prepare. While I thought my method was more fun, his clearly had the advantage of making sure we would stand a remote chance of being successful.

One of the requests of the Rally staff was to keep quiet for a while to allow those who were dealing with the disappointment of not being selected a chance to process it without listening to the cheers of others. This gave us some time to digest what we had signed up for. We had a few weeks before we had to send in our acceptance letter along with half of the entry fee. While I was still somewhat conflicted, I was genuinely happy for Terry. There was no way I was going to be the stick in the mud that decided we weren't going to compete. We mailed the check. We were committed.

He plunged into planning with a level of excitement I hadn't expected. He bought a bulletin board onto which he put slogans, calendars, and task lists. He researched what other rallies were occurring over the next year. SPANK, a five-day rally, was in August, only two months away. It would be a great opportunity for practicing a multi-day event. There were spaces available and he signed us up, wanting to ride as much as possible over the following year in preparation for the IBR. I kept nodding my head in agreement, telling Terry I thought his ideas were great, but inside I was terrified. I had yet to build the confidence to believe we could actually be successful. Terry, on the other hand, had no doubts.

Terry's planning highlighted my laziness. He wanted us to ride incessantly. I wanted to do some rides and hope for the best. Of course I knew better but I felt overloaded with information and stressed for balance in our lives. I wasn't sure I wanted to devote a full year getting ready to ride. More specifically, I wasn't sure I wanted to devote a full year to all the annoying details we needed to address to be prepared for an eleven-day rally.

Terry's lists were never ending. He had lists for bike maintenance and preparation that included reevaluating almost every single part of what to me seemed to be a perfectly fine motorcycle. A separate list focused on rallies—riding the '06 and '07 1088s, the SPANK rally, and then creating rides on our own to practice timing, efficiency, and teamwork. As if that weren't enough, there were lists detailing our physical preparations, which included working out with personal trainers and running half marathons. Squeezed in between all this were work, family, and running a household. I wasn't feeling the love.

Terry tackled his lists with a vengeance while I ignored mine. He wanted to improve the suspension on the bike for a smoother ride and better handling, which involved changing the rear shock absorber and the front forks. The shock that worked so well on the RT wasn't available for the Wing, and after researching the options, he chose a different company and shipped off the stock one to be replaced. He had work done on the front forks. Trying one company, he was never quite satisfied with their performance, sending them back for adjustments several times before giving up and going elsewhere. Each time he had to take the bike apart, which took valuable time away from other things at home. He rethought every aspect of the motorcycle, its performance, and its capacity to carry all the gear we would need. The Gold Wing had a built-in radio and speakers, and while we listened to music on occasion, we did so through speakers wired into our helmets. We used the same speakers for our intercom system, allowing us to talk with each other while riding. Terry found space by removing both of the front speakers. He put the Smart Tire monitor on one side so he could check the tire pressure on the go, and made a cubby for our rain gloves out of the other. Every inch was inspected for efficiency.

I finally showed an interest when he moved to details I cared about, ones that affected me more directly. We began analyzing our clothing, seeing what worked best and took up the least space in our small saddlebags. We put an MSR Dromedary bag, or water bladder, in the trunk, and drilled a hole for a hose that hooked onto the backpack. The Rally would be using Polaroid cameras, so Terry ordered a second one for a backup, and stocked up on film. We bought a small digital camera to carry with us for miscellaneous pictures. Every change or improvement required testing, and taking rides to see how it worked in real time.

I preferred being the social butterfly, the cheerleader, and the big-picture person. Terry focused on details and the small picture. While we mostly complemented each other, we also frustrated each other. If Terry pushed me, I rebelled. If something was high on my agenda, but not Terry's, the roles reversed. I offered helpful suggestions and he resisted. What set our relationship apart from any we had previously known was our ability to step back and see what was happening. Irritation became a signal that we needed to stop, "sit on the curb," and figure out a better way to accomplish our task. Terry put a sign on the bulletin board:

GOALS:

Have fun
Finish
Gold Medal

We took our goals seriously. They reflected deeper core values that nothing was more important to us than us. We agreed to withdraw from the IBR before it damaged our partnership. There's an old joke that goes, "How do you get to Carnegie Hall?" "Practice, practice, practice." We practiced, not just our rallying, but our marriage. Dealing with hard problems, sitting down and talking them through even when we didn't want to, and focusing on what mattered had already built a trust and deepened our commitment to each other. Feeling safe talking about our fears and dreams, and being able to be candid about our limitations, had created an intimacy that helped us through some really tough times. I could now be honest with Terry and tell him that I hated all the preparations, all the time it was taking to get ready for the IBR, and he could be honest that he felt pressure to make sure everything went well. Our openness created space for us to work out our resistance, to find ways to support rather than criticize each other for what we were feeling. Over time, because I was permitted to get there in my own way, I became increasingly invested in the process, and increasingly excited about riding in the Rally.

CHAPTER ELEVEN

SPANK

We talked about ways to improve our efficiency, and how I could be a more active participant in our rallies. One discovery concerned Terry and food. During the '06 1088, he was abrupt and irritated with me at a gas stop. It was very uncharacteristic and I commented on it, wondering if perhaps he was hungry. After eating a snack his outlook improved significantly, and I began to track his behavior. There was a definite correlation between hunger and irritation. I noticed other indicators of his moods. He'd shake his head, as if flicking off a bug, but I could tell he was getting tired and needed a piece of gum—the motion of chewing helped revive him. Slow answers to my questions, and small signs of confusion over directions, meant he was really tired and needed to sleep. I commented that his attraction to higher-carb meals might be causing the drowsiness. When he removed those from his diet he felt a significant difference. I began to read traffic signs out loud at night so Terry could keep his concentration on the road. I was another set of eyes watching for animals lurking on the sides of the highways, just waiting to leap out in front of us. I was helping more with routing, simple navigation, and strategizing, becoming less of a passenger and more of a partner.

At the 2006 Utah 1088 barbeque at Steve Chalmers's house, George Zelenz was chatting with a group of riders about one of the benefits of having a passenger. "If I had a pillion, I'd get her a GPS so she could be busy routing while I'm driving," he said. These were probably the most useful words spoken to us in our early years of rallying. Prior to this we had one GPS unit, which sat in front of Terry. To add another destination we had to stop, or Terry had to enter the data while riding, not the safest method. With a second GPS I could program in different locations, evaluate whether it made sense to change our route, or find hotels or gas stations using some of the other features of the unit.

After the 1088, we bought a second Garmin 2610. Terry urged me to read manuals and learn how to use it. I, of course, frustrated him by refusing to even look at a single book or the unit itself. He wanted me to learn various technical aspects of our riding, and I rebelled. He brought out gadgets and tried to explain them to me, and I changed the subject. What we finally realized is that I don't learn the way Terry does, and no matter how much we wanted me to be proficient at something, it wasn't going to be by studying a book. It was only when I saw the value in real time, and could play with something over and over, that I became comfortable and competent with it. With the GPS, that occurred during the 2006 SPANK rally.

The SPANK Rally was our first experience of a multi-day event, and my first experience of any rally besides the Utah 1088. It started in Gerlach, Nevada, a one-horse town in the middle of the Black Rock Desert area, about a hundred miles north of Reno. I'd never been there before and had no idea what to expect. Terry, as usual, handled all the bike preparations, including taking the Wing in for servicing just before we left home. He figured out a way to provide power to the backpack so I could have easy access to my GPS unit, as well as wiring in the iPod for music. My tasks were more home focused. I made sure the newspapers and mail were stopped, the bills were prepaid, cat care was covered, and the kids knew how to get in touch with us should something come up. I loaded the iPod with our favorite music and shopped for snack foods. We packed our own saddlebags after making list upon list to cover anything we thought we might need. The Rally ended in Colorado Springs, Colorado, and the 2006 IBA National Meet started the next morning in Denver, so our packing had to include anything we'd need for the three days we'd be spending there and the 1300-mile ride home. We knew we would get a T-shirt for participating in both events, and I counted on those to add to my meager wardrobe. This would be all I had available for the next two weeks, and it filled every inch of space I had.

> Personal Items Packing list (Lynda)
> 2 sets: (1 packed/1 wearing)
> Bike shorts
> Technical shirt
> Sports bra
> Socks (4)
> Underwear (4)
> Personal items/meds:
> 12 nights / 12 days meds
> Inhaler
> Homeopathic anti-inflammatory
> Deodorant, toothbrush, toothpaste
> Sunscreen, razor, refills (3)
> Tweezers/eye liner/mascara
> Hairbrush
> Inflatable neck pillow
> Thermal shirt
> Thermal leggings
> Gerbing pants

Gerbing jacket
Gerbing socks
Gerbing gloves
Midweight gloves
Lightweight gloves
Neck scarves: light, heavy
Sun/rain hat
Tennis shoes
Hiking shorts

Packing for SPANK and the National Meet. (Photo courtesy of Minou White)

We left in the early evening, hoping to break up the 680-mile ride by stopping somewhere south of Portland that night. Everything was running great as we rode down Highway 18 and turned onto I-5. About fifty miles into the ride, the "Check ABS" light came on. Although this had been a common occurrence with our BMW, it had never happened on the Wing. Neither of us had reason to panic, but we decided to stop at the next rest area to check it out. As Terry applied the brakes exiting the freeway he heard a strange noise and felt a *clunk*. When we pulled to a stop, the brake caliper was hanging by the brake line, unbolted from the front wheel. The mechanic who serviced the bike failed to tighten it correctly, and the bolt fell off somewhere on the freeway. Luckily, the line hadn't jammed into the wheel as we were stopping or it might have caused a serious problem. I was a bit freaked out to imagine what could have happened, but surprisingly, we were both able to focus on fixing the problem and continuing on. Terry jury-rigged a temporary solution and we kept riding, but we now had to find a dealer with the correct bolt to repair the bike.

We stopped for the night in the next town, and in the morning we pulled out our Gold Wing Rider's book to search for dealers. We called several, and despite learning that the service manual required that the bolt be replaced every time it was removed, apparently no one ever did so. As a result, the part we needed wasn't routinely kept in stock. We finally found a shop that had a bolt that would at least let us finish the ride to Gerlach. Terry called a dealer in Reno to overnight the Honda bolt so he could pick it up once we were in Nevada. I contained my anger at our dealer for putting our safety in jeopardy. Things don't always go according to plan, and the most important part was to figure out how to let go of my anger since there was nothing we could do at that moment, and holding on to it would only interfere with my focus during the rally.

We arrived in Gerlach and met up with the other riders. Some we knew from the 1088 and others we got to know for the first time. George Zelenz, the Rally Master, greeted us, and we said we had followed his advice and bought a second GPS. We relaxed Thursday evening, hung out at Bruno's Country Club—a name that makes it sound far fancier than the funky bar, restaurant, and motel it is—and settled into our room. Friday morning we went through technical inspection and the odometer check, and in general got ready for the starting banquet and the rally itself. In the afternoon Terry headed to Reno to get the bolt, a 200-mile round trip I elected to skip.

While he was gone, I went with a group of riders to Guru Lane, several miles outside of town. This was my first experience visiting the mishmash of odd artworks and tributes. The others explained its significance as a memorial site in the long-distance motorcycling community as we walked up the long dirt path. We arrived at the well-tended Iron Butt Association circle surrounded by various tokens of IBA certified rides and events, including a wooden pole with the names of all past Iron Butt Rally winners. The most moving part of the site was the middle, where there were stones laid out, each bearing the name of a fallen rider. I had ridden out on the back of Al Ladner's FJR. It was his first visit, as well, and I felt a bond with him as we shared this experience. Sadly, his name is now one of those carved on a stone, having lost his life a few years later in a motorcycling accident. I think of Al and our ride together every time I go there.

"Uncle Bud" Yates was a late arrival to the banquet, rushing in to explain that trying to catch a Gold Wing as it was tipping over was not a good idea—he had a bruised knee to prove it. Apparently he had stopped somewhere, lost his balance, and thrown his leg out in an attempt to keep the bike upright. "Next time, just let it fall," was his advice. I don't remember much else about him, but I always think about his suggestion when we're on the Wing.

Our bonus packs and flags were handed out after dinner. This was our first time using a flag in a rally. It had to be in every photo we took, with our number, 12, clearly visible. Grabbing our packets, Terry and I rushed to our room, this time using a computer to find locations and plan our route. Terry entered destinations, finding each location manually in a mapping program called Streets and Trips. He then color-coded each bonus with flag markers indicating their point value. The ride to the Kanab entrance to Zion National Park in Utah, and the Four Corners National Monument at the intersection of Colorado, New Mexico, Arizona, and Utah, were obvious choices because of their high point values. We discussed them in detail but opted not to go there because doing a long, boring, basically straight ride for only two bonuses didn't fit our style. We instead plotted a very interesting route through Northern California, over the Sierras, and down into Joshua Tree, the location of the checkpoint thirty-six hours later. With our plan in hand, we tried our best to go to sleep.

George threw a curveball into the rally plans in the morning by tossing in a few new bonuses, but it was obvious they weren't worth considering. Terry and I had our route, and we were set to execute on it. We took off south towards Reno, grabbed our first bonus, and turned west. On paper, our route was challenging but not impossible, taking us to some interesting locations in California. What looked simple on paper proved far more complex in reality. Montgomery Woods State Reserve, northwest of Ukiah, was on a tiny backroad that got narrower and narrower with every mile. We were wondering if we had taken a wrong turn when we finally came upon one of several signs for the park. We had no idea which sign George wanted, and the one in the bonus listing was nowhere to be found. We'd never faced this dilemma on the 1088 and weren't exactly sure how to proceed. We took pictures of every possible sign we found, and wasted far too much time trying to prove we had been there.

We backtracked on the same goat trail we had come in on and headed into Napa Valley, the home of traffic jams, tourists, and wineries. Our task was to find a specific small restaurant and order and photograph their French onion soup and *pomme frites* (French fries). We arrived to find a lovely, trendy little bistro filled with well-dressed diners waiting for tables. We were in full gear, gritty from our trek in the mountains, and only interested in ordering a meal so we could take a picture of it with our flag. This was not a drive-through, take-out-type restaurant so we politely talked our way into finding space at the bar and asked the staff if they would be so kind as to rush our order. Meanwhile, we invited quite a few stares and finally some fun conversations. In an "It's a small world" moment we mentioned that while the wineries in Napa were great—we'd visited there a year before— they weren't any better than those in Washington State where we lived. It turned out the woman sitting next to us owned one of our favorite Seattle wineries, which at that time only opened to the public twice a year. She made sure we were on their private invitation list and urged us to come by. We promised we would, and that we'd shower first next time. With some quick bites of our food, and our picture in hand, we headed off for Davis and the University of California. Somewhere on campus there was an egg waiting to be photographed.

Exhaustion hit after I scrambled all around the building in Davis trying to find the egg sculpture, ran back to the bike for the film I'd forgotten to load in the camera, and returned again for the flag I'd forgotten had to be in the photo. Finally Terry went back the third time to get the picture. We were starting to make dumb mistakes, costing us time and increasing our frustration. It was not yet nightfall, so we decided to find a hotel, get some decent rest, and resume riding after dark. Throwing off just enough gear to be able to sleep comfortably, we were out in seconds, only to be brought rudely back to awareness by the Screaming Meanie a short two hours later.

Quickly back on the bike, heading south on Hwy 99, we passed a rider who pulled off the freeway at a dark off-ramp. Recognizing the spare fuel cell on the bike—a common modification to a long-distance bike—we both assumed he was one of ours. If he was in the Rally, was there a bonus at that exit we had missed? That question surfaces every time we meet up with a fellow rider. What route are they riding? Is it better than ours? Did they see something in the rally packet we overlooked? Shaking off comparisons was challenging, but it was essential to bring our attention back to our ride, our plan, and our rally. Playing "what if" would only mess with our heads. It helped that moments later we both looked up to see shooting stars, probably dozens of them, across the night sky. On the motorcycle, with a full panorama available and no car roof blocking my view, I leaned back and watched the meteor shower unfold. It took my breath away, and it was hard not to stop and just take it all in.

Turning east, we began our mountain ascent on a steep, twisty road. It was slow going because we wanted to be safe and watch for animals, especially deer, suddenly darting out of the dark. I had a sense of deja vu. I had camped in this area in high school and college with friends, my first introduction to the Sierras. Memories of campfires, swimming in the creeks, hiking and partying came flooding in. The smells, the trees, all took me back to good times so many years before. I wanted to stop and show Terry all my old haunts, but time wouldn't allow it. I had to be content telling him stories as we turned onto a side road near one of the campgrounds I had stayed in. I was grateful to able to spend a few moments back in such familiar territory.

We returned to the main road, in the cold and dark, and a few miles later found the cutoff for Sherman Pass. We twisted and turned up what seemed to be a never-ending series of switch-backs, climbing higher and higher, finally reaching the 9200-foot summit just as the sun was beginning to rise. We stopped for awhile, taking in the view of the Owens Valley in the distance, the sun peeking through the trees, and appreciated how lucky we were to be in such a beautiful setting.

Just then another rider, Greg Marbach, appeared, jumped off his bike, took the required photo, and engaged us in a brief conversation. He hopped back on his bike and headed east down the mountain pass to the valley below. I turned to Terry and asked him if he thought Greg was doing OK, if he seemed tired, and if we should we have said or done something. Not knowing Greg well, we weren't sure if he would successfully monitor himself. Feeling slightly uncomfortable, but also freezing cold and wanting to re-hook up our electrics, we got back on the bike and took off in the same easterly direction. Barely half a mile later we saw a bike on the side of the road and my heart skipped a beat. I quickly realized the bike was on its side stand, and Greg was sleeping next to it on the hillside. Later he told us cars kept stopping to see if he was OK, and he finally had to continue further down the road to find a better place to nap where he wouldn't be constantly awakened by well-meaning drivers.

We were, despite the grueling ride through the mountains, ahead of schedule, and decided to add a few bonuses in the Los Angeles area. I grew up in L.A., wasn't intimidated by the traffic, and was even more excited by the possibility of adding to our score. Our first stop was a Thai restaurant, another attempt by George to have us try an eatery he really liked. Once again we had to order something and take our picture of the food alongside our flag. Unfortunately, while this restaurant was more of a fast-food, take-out place, the service was anything but fast. They were just opening for the day and nothing was ready. We picked something we thought would be quick to prepare, and also, to be true to the spirit of the requirements, we actually waited to have it fully cooked. Neither of us was hungry and we kept offering to buy someone's lunch, but I don't think anyone understood enough English to comprehend what we were asking. After a torturous twenty minutes, we ate two bites of the delicious meal and took our photo before reluctantly tossing the leftovers in the trash.

Traffic, as usual, was heavy as we headed downtown but the law in California allows lane splitting, or technically, lane sharing. This meant Terry and I could ride between the lines of cars as they inched along, a giant behemoth of a motorcycle in a very narrow space. We had never done it before, and Terry told me to hold still as he moved out of our lane and passed within a hair of the motorists on either side of us. It was a bit unnerving, but also liberating to be able to keep moving rather than fretting that our water-cooled engine would overheat in stop-and-go traffic. Our next stop, a picture in front of the Walt Disney Concert Hall, was an easy one, and we were quickly headed east towards Hemet.

The mountain-road riding the night before was starting to take its toll on Terry. I noticed his answers to my questions were becoming abrupt and his mood was irritable. The heat was getting to us, and the surface streets, filled with stoplights and late-afternoon traffic, were slowing our progress. When we arrived at the Maze Petroglyph, our next bonus, he told me he couldn't get back on the bike and needed to nap. As I sat in the full heat of the day, not a single tree for shade, I felt myself getting frustrated that he couldn't keep going. Terry wanted us to be aggressive and competitive, but the reality of his need for sleep kept hitting us in the face. We'd constantly discuss what he wanted to do versus what I believed we really could do. Terry would accuse me of doubting him and I would accuse him of having eyes bigger than his stomach, a favorite expression of my dad's, meaning he always thought he could do more than he could. The tricky part is neither of us was always right, and we never knew when to listen to which one of us. I knew I could be too cautious, and sometimes Terry really could do more than I thought. Reluctantly, I sat quietly while he slept, knowing it was the right thing to do but hating it nonetheless. When he awakened, we started off for our next bonus, which would take us over the San Jacinto Mountains and down into Palm Desert. We were fully committed to the route when we came upon a blockade due to a fire that had broken out farther along the road. It was now closed to all vehicles, no exceptions.

The rules for a rally state that when a road is closed if there is another way to get into the location, no matter how far out of the way it is, then the bonus is considered good and you have to ride to it. If it is the only road in and it's closed, you merely have to take a picture of the closed sign with your flag in the photo. Luck was not on our side. The road we were planning to take ended in Palm Desert, and the bonus we were trying to reach was attainable by going up from the desert side. This meant we'd not only have to backtrack and go down a twisty mountain road to intersect with I-10, but we'd have to ride through Palm Springs, a popular tourist town, at 5 p.m. on a Friday night. We'd also be taking our chances that the road really was open far enough to get the photo. This was an example of Terry wanting to push but me knowing the area well enough to know it wasn't worth the effort because the heat and traffic would wear us out. He kept insisting we not give up, and I kept insisting there was no way we'd do it. I finally won the argument, but only after we rode through endless miles of small, two-lane mountain road before even reaching I-10. Terry conceded he was too tired. We set our GPS to the bonus in the Salton Sea, took the necessary photo, and headed for the checkpoint in Joshua Tree.

We gathered all our photos, receipts and rally pack and sat down for scoring. Going bonus by bonus, we held our breath as our items were examined to see if we met all the requirements. We were pleased when we were awarded all the points we had turned in. We were also pleased with the chances we had taken and the aggressiveness of our ride. We spoke with a few of the riders who had gone to the Four Corners and who told us they had had plenty of time to sleep along the way. They were frustrated with a scoring decision George made—they thought they had correctly answered a question regarding a sign, but George disagreed. In all rallies, however, it is the Rally Master who makes the final decisions, and arguing will usually only result in a disqualification. They had no choice but to abide by George's ruling, and in any case, they were all well rested for Leg Two. We, on the other hand, were exhausted. Our hard work had paid off, putting us in second place for Leg One, but we were soon to find out it had cost us dearly.

CHAPTER TWELVE

Perspective

We started our next leg of route planning tired, and made several poor decisions as a result. I was stubborn about where I was willing to ride. After feeling somewhat tricked by the roads we had taken in the first leg, I didn't believe it would get any easier now and basically threw out any road that I thought might be too difficult. I did not want to go to Utah since we had ridden there so recently in the 1088. Terry and I had been to New Mexico the previous spring on a vacation with our kids, but had only seen part of the state. When we saw a lot of bonuses there, we mapped out a route that would let us visit the places we hadn't yet been. We planned our route emotionally and exhausted, and we deferred to my need for caution. The impact of those decisions wouldn't be obvious until much later in the rally.

George added a unique feature to this leg. It included increasing or decreasing point values for a bonus depending on the day you got it. Bonuses that were easy to get had lower point values, but if you had to backtrack to get it, or if it was really far out of the way, it might be worth more on a given day. Trying to figure out which bonuses to get was challenging enough—now we had to factor in timing over several days. In addition, George created an efficiency bonus for the least miles ridden with the most points obtained within a specific six-hour window. The idea was to get within striking distance of a high-point bonus, get a gas receipt, go to the bonus and return to the same gas station if possible, riding the least number of miles. We planned to combine Los Alamos for the gas receipt with the Bandolier National Monument bonus, a distance of perhaps six miles. We'd leave Joshua Tree in California, head east through Arizona picking up bonuses scattered along I-10, get everything we could in New Mexico, and head for the finish in Colorado Springs, Colorado. Even in our exhaustion, the plan felt solid and attainable.

Making quick work of Arizona, we headed into New Mexico. George's sense of humor was apparent in one of the first bonuses we went after once we crossed into the state. We had to determine a location based on GPS coordinates, which meant putting the longitude and latitude numbers George had given us into the unit and see where it took us. The instructions said we would find a message somewhere along the roadside. We easily found the GPS coordinates and spotted a large, unremarkable sign. Walking around to the back we noticed something had been painted out. We could barely made out the words "Set phasers to SPANK," clearly the work of our Rally Master. We called George to let him know it had been obliterated by evil forces and that we could only take a photo of the damaged remains, which he said was fine for scoring the bonus.

We continued along the two-lane road and discovered we were almost out of fuel. It hadn't occurred to us that the tiny towns on our map were too small to have gas stations. I used the GPS to try and find one, but found the closest station would be just beyond the capacity of our tank, or at least as low as we had ever let it get. Terry slowed down and headed toward the interstate where we hoped we'd find an unlisted station to save us. We passed a border patrolman who confirmed that, no, there were no services along the road we were on, and wished us luck. Finally reaching the highway, Terry kept our speed under fifty miles per hour and drafted a safe distance behind slow-moving trucks to save every drop of gas he could. I imagined myself lighter, anything to help us go a few feet further. On our last fumes, we finally spotted an oasis in the desert. We were saved.

Our timing on subsequent stops kept improving, as did our luck. One bonus required taking a tour of the Acoma Pueblo, or Sky City, a Native American town built on top of a 367-foot sandstone mesa that has been continuously inhabited since AD 1100. We had to find and count the number of rainbows inside one of the buildings, an old chapel. We had no idea when, or how often, the tours were given. We arrived just as one was about to leave so Terry stripped off his Aerostich, threw on hiking shorts over his riding tights, and grabbed his tennis shoes while I bought him a ticket. The tours lasted a minimum of an hour, and there was really no way to get back to the Visitor's Center once it started. We learned their tours, and trams, only ran every few hours. We resigned ourselves to being grateful he made it on a tour as quickly as he did. He took off and all I could do was wait, watch the clock, and hope.

Barely thirty minutes later, he raced back into the center shouting, "I got the bonus, let's go!" We ran back to the bike and he put his gear on while explaining how he had made it back so fast. As luck would have it the chapel was one of the first stops on the tour, and, walking inside, he counted all the rainbows he could see from the entrance. For some reason, he walked in a bit farther, and upon turning to leave, saw one more rainbow above the balcony. Score! The tour guide offered to call a tram to take him back down to the Visitor's Center, and while he sat by the curb waiting for it, it suddenly dawned on him it would be faster if he just ran. That explained why he was completely out of breath when he came in, but the thirty or forty minutes he saved us paid off later that day.

Back on the bike, heading west, I began to play with the GPS. We were ahead of our timetable, and perhaps could add a few points if we could only figure out where. We hadn't planned on going to the Four Corners Monument, the bonus we had opted to skip in Leg One that was now available again in Leg Two, but I calculated adding it, and it was apparent we could get there just before it closed at sunset. It's located in a desolate area, without any nearby services, including hotels. If we got there too late, it would be a wasted trip. Keeping a steady pace, we arrived in time and were surprised to be greeted by tourists who wondered what our number was and what our next bonus was going to be. We found out a few other riders had been there shortly before us and had briefly explained what we were all doing. The tourists mentioned two riders in particular who "both had the number six." We cracked up, knowing they were Tobie and Lisa Stevens, a husband-and-wife team riding separate bikes whose numbers were actually six and nine.

While we were elated to have added an unexpected bonus, and a high-point one at that, we realized the cost of our hasty planning back in Joshua Tree. By going so far east early in the rally, we had limited our ability to get bonuses. We were going to exhaust what was available in New Mexico before we ran out of time, and were now going to be in the undesirable position of arriving in Colorado Springs too early. No matter how we tried to reconfigure our route, the result was the same. I was mad at myself for excluding Utah and had a hard time letting it go. Terry did his best to point out we had both made the decision, and it was based as much on wanting to ride in New Mexico as in avoiding Utah. Rallying wasn't only about winning, it was also about having a positive experience. Perhaps had we not been so high in the standings after the first leg I might have been kinder to myself, but I felt like we had failed to live up to what we had already accomplished. I have this argument inside my head many times. I knew what Terry was saying was true, yet I struggled with putting expectations on myself and on us.

A good night's sleep usually helps snap me out of my doldrums, and once again I awoke refreshed and ready to tackle the new day. Our plan was to get Chaco Culture National Historic Park and then head to Los Alamos for the efficiency bonus. Chaco is one of the densest and most exceptional concentrations of ancient pueblos in the Southwest, and sits basically in the middle of nowhere. Our GPS and the rally pack had us approaching Chaco from the south. The GPS, in its usual wisdom, often told us to turn where no roads existed. We had learned to ignore it when what it was telling us to do made no sense. When it finally told us to turn north on a sketchy dirt road, we stopped, checked it out, and pulled out our computer and paper maps. We could see another road that led to Chaco, but from the north. We decided to ride a few miles out of our way to the next town and ask a local which road we should take.

That turned out to be an excellent decision. He pointed us to the northern route, and off we went. The first ten miles were nicely paved, and then we hit thirteen miles of dirt, gravel and washboard. Terry is not a dirt-bike rider, and I kept reminding him to relax and breathe, noticing him becoming tense and irritable. We slowed to twenty miles per hour to deal with all the ruts and bumps. About six miles in, we came across a sign that said "Do not cross if water is on the roadway" just before a concrete culvert that crossed a ditch with about three inches of water flowing over it. "Hold still," was all Terry said as we rode across. We both knew the risk was a flash flood from further upstream, but because it had not rained that day we took our chances. We finally arrived at the national park, where the road was of course now nicely paved. Another frustrating bonus, where we had no time to stop and see anything, just stamp a park emblem in our rally pack and go, back onto the torturous ride to the main highway.

Our GPS directed us to a shortcut for Los Alamos, where we would be in perfect position to start the efficiency bonus.

As we turned onto the road we both noticed the sign that said 'Impassible when wet." We debated the wisdom of taking such a road, but it hadn't rained and we assumed we'd be fine. We failed to consider that it had rained the past few nights and that the road might not have had time to dry out. When the road turned from pavement to hard-packed dirt, then softer dirt, and finally mud, we kept hoping we could tough it out. I held perfectly still and Terry navigated the conditions as best he could. Unfortunately, the front wheel hit a rock, the bike slipped out from under us, and down we went.

The mud was so thick it didn't hurt at all, and as I lay on the ground my only thought was should I take my gloves off to get up or leave them on? As silly as it sounds, I was seriously trying to decide if it'd be better to have muddy gloves or to put muddy hands into clean gloves. Terry just wanted me to hurry up and get off the bike to help right it again. The bike, fully loaded, weighs around 1000 pounds, and as we tried to right it the mud would suck it back down. It took both of us to lift it up, Terry pushing on one side and me pulling on the other. Once we got it upright, he tried to ride it forward but it slipped again in the ooze. While we debated what to do, a truck came from the opposite direction and stopped to see if we needed help. The driver told us the road remained bad for several more miles, which confirmed any doubts we had about our decision to turn around. I walked while Terry slowly rode the bike through the mud back onto the dirt road, where I remounted and we returned to the main highway.

I was frustrated. Our efficiency bonus was gone. The starting receipt had to be obtained at a specific time, and because of our mistake, we'd now have to get it in Cuba, a city almost a hundred miles from Bandolier instead of the six miles away in Los Alamos. Arriving at the gas station, we surveyed the bike and ourselves. Everything was covered in mud. Surrendering to our lot, we put our rally flag on the bike for fun and took some photos, and agreed to never explain anything to anyone in the rally who asked. Better to keep them guessing.

"…and down we went."

We took the main road over the hills towards Los Alamos, this one paved the entire way. As we started up the mountainside, the sky erupted in a torrential downpour. Terry could barely see the road and water gushed sideways from the hillside on our left to the cliffs on our right. The rain finally let up as we reached the top, and we began laughing. While still disappointed in our miscalculation on the previous road, our mood lightened.

The bonus in Bandolier was a mile-long hike into the Monument and a climb up three wooden ladders to a kiva high in the cliffs. Terry and I had been there the previous spring with our kids, so we knew what to expect. I'm afraid of heights and the climb was too exposed for my comfort, so Terry did the hike while I stayed with the bike and tried to dry some of our gear. I'm not sure how dry things got, but it felt good to have something to do while I waited. Once he returned we put our soggy gear back on and rode to the gas station in Los Alamos. We were greeted by Matt Watkins, another rider who was claiming the same combination we had hoped to get had we not detoured through the mud. He asked what had happened to us, and we just looked at him with innocent expressions. "What are you talking about? What mud?" He laughed and let it drop.

We chatted about what bonuses we had just completed, and we mentioned Chaco Cultural Center. He told us he was going to ride there the next day. Later we found out our strategy of silence had messed with his head when he tried to ride to Chaco from the south. When he started up the muddy road we had bypassed, he kept telling himself that if we could make it up there two-up on a Wing, he should be able to do it solo on an FJR, a much lighter and more agile bike. I believe he gave up after his third fall and his bike looked like a dead spider, wheels up in the air. It wasn't until the finisher's banquet that we told him the whole story.

We were greeted by George, the Rally Master, and several visitors when we arrived in Colorado Springs. We were told very quietly that there would be a riders-only meeting at the start of scoring, and we were asked not to go online or talk to anyone outside of the rally. We could tell something had happened, but couldn't imagine what. We only knew it couldn't be good.

As we assembled in the scoring room, Terry looked around and noticed Uncle Bud was missing. At that moment, George came in and in a voice breaking with emotion told us Uncle Bud had been killed in an accident earlier in the rally. We were stunned. George had not wanted us to know while we were still competing because he was worried it would get into our heads and perhaps cause one of us to lose focus and have an accident. My heart broke watching the anguish in George's face, and seeing how hard this news was on others who knew Uncle Bud personally. It was difficult to refocus on scoring knowing the pain others were feeling. During the finishers' banquet I spent quite a bit of time with the riders who had been with him at the time of the accident and listened to their stories. Once again, bonds were formed that run deep to this day.

Uncle Bud's death put rallying into perspective. We were reminded yet again that life was precious and to make sure we made time for our family and friends. We talked about whether this would affect our decision to ride or to rally. Giving up either might give us the illusion of being safe, but it would also mean giving up doing something we loved. We were both willing to keep practicing our skills and taking reasonable precautions, but we also knew life happens and sometimes it hurts. We'd lost friends to cancer, car accidents, plane crashes, and old age, and the way they had died hadn't diminished the pain of their loss. We wouldn't take unnecessary risks but we would keep riding.

We spent the next few days in Denver at the National Meet, where it helped to be with friends who understood the impact of Uncle Bud's death, and also why we kept riding. During the day we listened to seminars that now had more meaning for me after being in several rallies and completing several SaddleSore rides. At one IBA dinner we were asked, as participants in the next Iron Butt Rally, to stand, and it was both a strange and exciting feeling to receive applause from a group of our fellow riders. It was making everything start to seem more real.

One the way home from Colorado we analyzed our performance in our first multi-day rally. We had dropped from second to tenth place out of a total of nineteen riders who finished. We learned we could compete over several days, and in some ways I preferred the multi-day format since we were able to get more sleep than in a one-day rally. We gained valuable experience in routing, pacing, evaluating, and adding bonuses, and dealing with bad roads, weather, and exhaustion. We made some disastrous decisions and kept riding, finding our way through discouragement. We worked well together and had fun, and my role was expanding. Our preparations were starting to pay off, moving us one step closer to the big show, the Iron Butt Rally, the following August.

CHAPTER THIRTEEN

Practice, Practice, Practice

We had been together for over two years and our relationship had grown into an intimate partnership. We had integrated our families, created a home, learned to balance our needs, and shared some amazing adventures. Each ride we had taken taught us something, whether it was how to find agreement in the midst of misunderstanding, how to recover when things went off in unpredictable directions, or how to take the time to enjoy life's fragility. We learned to read each other and our moods. Terry knew when my anxiety might be driving the questions I asked, and I understood when his irritability was arising from a physical need, like hunger. We were functioning more and more seamlessly on and off the bike. It was time to put all we had learned to the test, turn up the volume, and push ourselves even further as we began preparing for the Iron Butt Rally. The Rally had started as Terry's dream, but now that I had jumped into it with both feet I was determined we'd be successful.

But despite my good intentions I still had no comprehension of the amount of work Terry was doing, how much time it took, or, to some extent, why it mattered. I supported the idea of planning, but I didn't take it as seriously. It was easy for me to map out a forty-eight-state ride, because in my mind that was going to be fun. I was OK shopping for clothes and trying them out to see what worked. I surprised Terry with a homemade rally flag for a ride we did to practice our picture taking. I was less tolerant of the time it took him each night to work in the garage. It sometimes felt to me like he was overanalyzing things, and that all these details would work out just fine. I recognized the differences in our personalities—he's a detail person and I'm not. I do best when paired with someone who remembers the little things, like wiring the iPod. I prefer to program music that would be fun to listen to, never thinking about how it might need to be recharged. Our teamwork became even more apparent as our preparations continued. I kept Terry from becoming too detailed, from overbuilding everything and running out of time, and he pushed me to tackle challenges I would have avoided.

One of Terry's best ideas was to run mini rallies to practice route planning, timing, and efficiency. The Washington chapter of the Gold Wing Road Riders Association has an annual fundraiser called Wing Washington that divides the state into five sections, with five things in each section to photograph with your bike in the picture. The types of places are the same in each section—such as a restaurant, a church, or a historical site. Riders can go at any time over the summer, and there's a banquet in the fall when you turn in your photos for raffle tickets. Action Motor Sports, a motorcycle shop in Beaverton, Oregon, sponsored a similar event called the Dam Tour. Riders take photos of eight dams in Oregon and eight in Washington, and four bonus dams in the greater Northwest. Terry had already plotted a ride along the Columbia River and the fourteen hydroelectric dams between Portland and Revelstoke, British Columbia. When he heard about the Dam Tour and one of the bonus dams was the last one on our route, he signed us up.

We schedule our Dam Ride for late April, hoping all the mountain passes would be clear and safe, and we invited our friend John Parrish to ride along with us. The purpose of this trip was to focus on photography and timing, so I asked my friend Linda to sew flags for us, while I surprised Terry and John by creating bonus sheets, mimicking the real ones we had used in rallies.

* *

Washington   4 points   Available daylight hours
John Day Dam

Take a photo of your bike in front of the dam sign. (if no dam sign is available, a photo of your bike with the dam in the background is sufficient.)

The John Day Dam is located along the Columbia River.

Time: _____ Odometer: _____ Code: JD

* *

We rode to Portland on Friday night after work and were on the road early Saturday morning, heading east on I-84 to Bonneville Dam, the last one on the Columbia River but the first one on our trip. We took pictures of the sign at each dam, remembering to have our flags in the photo and log the bonus. We practiced putting the log, camera, and flag away after each stop. Our goal was to complete the ride and make it back home by Sunday night, a distance of about 1400 miles. The biggest challenge was to make a remote ferry crossing before 11 p.m. on

Saturday because if we missed the ferry, we'd be sleeping in the freezing cold alongside the road in bear country.

The best roads were the ones we had never been on before, especially the ones after we left Grand Coulee, riding first up Cache Creek Road before taking Highway 21 to the Danville border crossing into Canada. It was a gorgeous ride through the countryside, with lazy sweeping curves along a river with mountains sometimes closing in on us and sometimes off in the background. John was a great companion, taking pictures of his flag alongside ours, and letting us lead the way and set the pace.

After entering Canada we decided to try the cell phone. Terry had just wired it into our intercom system so we could hear it directly in our helmets, and we were still figuring out how to use it. We gave commands to call our son Chris and it dialed the number. We talked for a short time and everything seemed to work well. About an hour later Terry happened to glance down and was stunned to see an empty phone holder. Reaching up under the shelf where the holder was still bolted on he found the phone hanging from the two cables, barely connected to the bike. Apparently a bump had caused the phone to separate from the double-lock tape holding it to the mount. We lost the battery cover in the process, but at least we still had the phone. At our next stop we once again brought out our trusty duct tape to create a more secure mount.

Riding this early in the season was difficult because we hadn't built up seat time or stamina, but we needed to push hard to made the ferry crossing in Galena, British Columbia, five hours north of the border on roads that had become increasingly technical as nightfall descended. I made myself useful by becoming another pair of eyes scouting for deer and elk hiding in the trees. We had a nearly full moon to help us see farther up the road, which we lit up even more brightly with our auxiliary lighting. We could see mountains in the distance and a lake shimmering alongside us in the moonlight, and could only imagine that the views were spectacular during daylight hours. John followed closely behind us as we made the ferry crossing with only minutes to spare.

We stayed overnight in Revelstoke, British Columbia, and once again woke up early to head to Mica Dam, a 90-mile ride one way with no services along the route. The road paralleled the river, rising and falling with the undulating hillside. Terry concentrated on the riding while I took in the incredible views of the surrounding mountains, still heavily covered in snow. We started the morning in a light rain, but as we approached Mica Dam the drizzle turned to snow. There were clumps of fog everywhere, lifting occasionally to give us only brief glimpses of the area. We stayed just long enough in the freezing cold to take our pictures before hustling the 90 miles back into town where we turned south to Seattle and the four-hundred-mile ride back home. When we submitted the picture of Mica Dam to Action Sports in Oregon, we apparently infuriated a few riders who were amazed we had attempted it so early in the season, and therefore beat them to getting it first. Unbeknownst to us, there had been quite a lot of chatter about this on the store's website and we had blithely waltzed in and cut the conversation short.

Pausing for a few minutes in the snow and fog at our final dam.

We spent the next month creating mini rallies, combining locations from Wing Washington and the Dam Tour. We printed each location on a separate strip of paper and put them into a hat. We printed random point values on different strips of paper and put those in another hat. We then decided how long our "rally" was going to be, either twelve or twenty-four hours, and which region of the state it would be in. The length of time and the destination determined how many bonuses we pulled out of the hat. Terry picked a bonus and a point value, matched them up, and that determined the bonus's worth. After we selected a designated number of bonuses, more than we could complete in our allotted time, we had our "rally pack." We'd argue about the best way to plan, the best route to take, and who had the best ideas, and learned how to work together under pressure. This was our best way of simulating routing on the clock, trying to come up with a route with the highest point value.

The benefit of doing this was to push ourselves to keep moving, to ride efficiently, and to learn where we ran into trouble. One of the biggest problems we discovered was dealing with exhaustion. It was on one of these mini rallies, stopping for yet another short break somewhere in eastern Washington, that we realized we actually spent more time getting on and off the bike to have a snack and try to wake ourselves up than if we had just pulled off the road and slept for thirty minutes. We got much better at determining the difference between the times when eating would revive Terry and when only sleeping would do.

In addition to all of our riding, we prepared ourselves physically for the rigors of an eleven-day rally. We would be on the bike for incredibly long hours, day after day. The wear and tear on our bodies would be intense. Backs, shoulders, legs, and knees would take a beating, even for me as the pillion. Core strengthening would help me hold myself upright and keep me from slouching. Terry's personal trainer gave him workouts specifically designed to strengthen parts of his body used in motorcycling. Running long distances would prepare us mentally for the exhaustion we would be facing. Anything that increased our stamina would pay off in the middle of the rally when we knew we still had days to go. Keeping our body weight as low as possible also helped the load on the bike, which with both of us and all our gear was already straining the recommended limits.

Endurance is as much mental as it is physical, and the decision to try running for hours at a time provided ample training in mindfulness. Running, which did not come naturally to me, was an excellent place to practice the mental focus I believed would be important in the Rally. Unlike Terry, I had not been a runner in my youth—in fact, quite the opposite. My mother smoked most of my childhood years, and I grew up in Los Angeles, one of the smoggiest cities in the country. I could barely run down my driveway without wheezing. I started running as an adult only to vary my aerobic routine, but had more fun taking spin classes than pounding a treadmill at the gym. Terry, who ran on his cross-country team in high school, had previously completed both a half and a full marathon.

In November of 2006, Terry ran the Seattle Half Marathon, while I planned to walk it with a few of my girlfriends. At the last minute, my flag-sewing friend Linda and I decided we'd try to run for at least some of the time, even though neither of us had ever run more than five miles in our lives. We ended up walking only three of the miles and running the other ten. I was sick for almost twenty-four hours afterwards, but I was inspired to fully commit to train for a run instead of backing my way into one. We chose the Vancouver, British Columbia, Half Marathon in May. Linda and I planned to run together while Terry, who ran at a much faster pace, would go on his own. The timing of this race fit perfectly with our plans for the IBR and the rides we had scheduled for the spring and early summer. I created a training schedule, which required me to run at least three times a week, and slowly increased my mileage until I could run ten miles. The theory is that if you can run ten miles, you should be able to cover the 13.1-mile distance without a problem. I struggled at times with wanting to quit, with hating the run, and with feeling like I couldn't take one more step. My body ached, and I'd keep checking my watch to see if I was close to the end. In those instances, when it was the worst, it'd seem like I was never close to finishing, and I had to find a way to keep going. Mentally it was very similar to what I had faced on some of our endurance rides.

In confronting these issues during my runs, I learned to find a way to keep my focus on the moment at hand, not to freak out about how far I still had to go, and to believe in myself.

We made a weekend getaway out of it, driving up to Canada Friday before the race and checking into our hotel. We walked around the city Saturday and picked up our race packets at the Expo, which reminded me of motorcycling rallies although on a much larger scale. Runners were everywhere, excitement was high, and it was hard to get to sleep while anticipating the early wake-up the next morning. When we arrived at the starting line under a light drizzle I was surprisingly calm. I realized I was ready. I had trained well, and knew I would be able to run the whole time, which I did. As I crossed the finish line, I felt an elation similar to what I felt after the first Utah 1088, a sense of accomplishment that I could run for two-and-a-half hours and not die. I was pleased with how my body felt—tired, sore, and strong.

Terry and I were already signed up to participate in the Seattle Half Marathon the following November as part of our training schedule, which ensured we would maintain our stamina for August. Continuing to work with our personal trainers would keep us accountable for our strength training. More important, we both were practicing strategies for enduring hours of hard work, coming back from exhaustion, and staying positive even when we were worn out.

CHAPTER FOURTEEN

The Lower Forty-Eight

O ur major training ride was a 48-10 ride in late May, taking advantage of the extra vacation time over the Memorial Day weekend and giving us our longest continuous riding experience to date. The IBA certifies several variations of this ride. At its most basic the goal is to to obtain an electronically generated receipt from each of the contiguous forty-eight states within a ten-day time frame.

48 States-10 Days Rules

NOTE: You must be familiar with Iron Butt Association documentation requirements before attempting this ride. Carefully review the SaddleSore 1000 requirements before riding. Only the most seasoned riders should attempt this ride.

Riders attempting to obtain certification for riding to 48 States in 10 Days ride (ride to all 48 continental United States of America) must adhere to the following rules:

You may take any route you wish to all 48 states, however the following is required:

In each State, you must ride to a city, town or community and document your visit (i.e., picture of "Welcome to State" sign is not acceptable).

Obtain a dated business receipt showing the name of city, town or community along with the STATE (this information should be pre-printed or computer generated, not hand written) and the business name. Most gasoline station receipts are acceptable.

Make a log entry showing date, time and odometer reading for each receipt.

Include a basic map of your route (an old map marked up is fine) so that we can follow your route.

Preparation for the Start:

In order to document your ride, the Iron Butt Association requires that you obtain at least **TWO** eyewitnesses to document the start of your ride. Witnesses for the basic 48 States in 10 Days may be a friend (but not one on the ride with you), spouse or even gas station attendant willing to answer a letter from the IBA about your start or end time.

Make sure that you inform potential witnesses that the Iron Butt Association may be auditing certain aspects of your ride and may be sending them a letter with a copy of the page they signed asking them to verify the information provided. Keep in mind that a witness who doesn't bother to respond to an audit letter is as good as having no witness at all! To this extent, it is highly recommended that you send a thank you note to all of your witnesses after you complete your ride. Besides, many of them will be waiting to hear how you did.

Try to remember that you must act as a salesperson each time you approach someone to sign your log. If someone doesn't want to provide their home address - suggest they give a business address. According to experienced riders, taking a few minutes to explain your ride to potential witnesses will get them involved. Most people will actually feel honored to sign your witness form. However, attitude plays a key role, if someone refuses to sign your book, don't argue, move on to the next person.

Obtain a start receipt with Date, Time and location printed on it.

* * * This will be your official starting time * * *

Along the route, the following log entries and completed witness forms are mandatory:

Log entries must be made at each gas stop. A receipt must accompany each logbook entry.

Log entries must be made at every rest stop over 1 hour along the route and should include beginning and ending times. Meals are considered rest stops - obtain restaurant receipts where possible.

Toll Roads and Toll Bridges; if you pay electronically, please note it on your application so we can request the account data if needed. For those that pay with cash, where possible, grab a receipt, they are great sources to help support your ride claim.

The Finish: obtain a time/dated receipt showing location.

* * * This will be your official ending time * * *

While there are published routes other riders have taken, I chose to figure one out on my own, and had a lot of fun coming up with a plan. The challenge was to make sure to get every state while riding the fewest miles for the overall trip.

Our ride started in Kennewick, Washington, near the home of our friend Matt Watkins. We spent the evening visiting with a group of motorcycling friends who all signed our witness papers and wished us well. Knowing we needed a good night's sleep, we declined the offer of a guest room at Matt's house and headed to a local hotel for our early morning departure. Our planned route took us to Oregon, east to Utah, south through Nevada and a corner of California. It then turned east, zigzagging through the southern part of the country, snaking up the east coast, and then once again west through the northern states, finishing in eastern Montana. Traditionally, the ride is easier in the west because of the open roads and higher speeds on the interstates.

The ride from Washington to Utah was a familiar one, the same route we took when going to the 1088. It starts with a bit of twisty mountain road in Oregon and is then followed by endless miles of grazing lands through Idaho and northern Utah, broken up only by a few major cities and a lot of small, one-gas-station towns. Turning south towards Salt Lake I was reminded of the contrast between the beautiful Wasatch Mountains to the east and the ugliness of the urban sprawl at their feet. Commercial buildings, strip malls, and housing developments consumed the spaces on either side of the interstate until well past Provo, when we once again encountered open ranch lands. We arrived in Las Vegas late at night, ready for our first hotel, a dingy Days Inn filled with slot machines and smokers. Leaving Vegas as quickly as we could the following morning, we had only to dip into California far enough for a receipt before turning east and into Arizona.

Riding into New Mexico was beautiful after the barrenness of eastern Arizona. The interstate was lined with red rock mesas as it swept down towards Albuquerque, and it took us past some of the places we had visited the summer before on the SPANK rally. Stopping for the night in the northwest corner of Texas, we were already on the bike when the sun peeked up over the fields, a blazing orange orb of intensity. My pictures could never fully capture the panoramas we saw, and we didn't want to take the time to stop to see if I could get better ones. I had to be content with breathing in the beauty and observing the day as it unfolded, once again unfettered by a roof over my head or air warmed to the perfect temperature.

We ran into our first problem early on coming into Colorado, where we intended to stop in a small town near the border and quickly head east. Arriving early in the morning, I ran inside the only open store, a mom-and-pop diner. I was greeted by the locals gossiping over their morning coffee and an ancient register that didn't produce receipts of any kind. It was clear they wouldn't have what I needed but I chatted for a few moments, not wanting to seem rude. A quick recalculation on the GPS showed a larger town another thirty miles farther into the state, from where we could take smaller roads across Kansas before dipping back down into Oklahoma.

I was surprised by the geology of northern Oklahoma. I had somehow pictured flat fields stretching endlessly toward the horizon, but instead we were greeted by rolling hills as we rode across the state and on into Missouri. The small, two-lane roads were brutally rough, and the abrupt jolts from the pavement were pounding Terry's arms and hands. The GPS and radar detector were mounted on a bar that spanned the handlebars of the bike, and the vibration caused by their weight was reverberating throughout Terry's body. As we heading south through Arkansas, the pain became unbearable, and we finally had to stop to find a temporary fix before we could continue further.

An elderly man wandered over to chat while Terry moved the equipment to different locations on the bike. The man asked about the bike and where we were from. I don't think I've ever spoken with anyone who talked as slowly, pausing in-between every word for what seemed like minutes. I could tell Terry wanted to focus on fixing the bike, so I kept answering the man's questions, diverting his attention, trying to be friendly and engaging. He had never been more than a few miles from his home in his entire life, and was struggling to believe that we could have come over 3000 miles in only three days. He drew the words out, over and over, "Three thousand miles in three days!" as if the constant repetition would suddenly make it more comprehensible. It was the kind of moment, unplanned and memorable, that happened often when we were on the bike. Somehow, people were more willing to approach us, a couple sharing a single motorcycle, and pepper us with questions that they might never ask if we were in a car.

The long distances gave me a lot of time to think. Reflecting on the past two years, I was surprised how comfortable I had become with silence. When we first started riding, I wanted music playing almost constantly. Terry had a mini CD player with only a few discs that he would play repeatedly, driving me crazy. Adding the iPod gave us a much wider variety of music, and appealed to my shorter attention span, letting me switch from song to song as the mood struck. Singing along to the music, with my intercom in mute mode, I'd even dance to some of my favorites, entertaining myself and keeping the blood flowing as I sat mile upon mile. I worked out an exercise routine, using the resistance against the wind as I'd push my arms, pretending I was lifting weights. I convinced myself it was helping me stay in shape.

Terry often suggested waiting before turning the iPod on, especially early in the morning, and at first I wasn't sure what to do. The scenery was often breathtaking, but it could also be monotonous and sometimes even ugly. It felt like I was simply counting the minutes until he agreed to add sound and save me. But as the miles added up, I noticed I had found a relationship with myself I hadn't previously known. The quiet inside my head became my companion, and my thoughts had the time and space to float freely. A place would trigger a series of memories, and I'd find myself lost in images of childhood, vacations, or friends. New places inspired me to imagine the lives of the people who lived there, what they did, how their days unfolded. I thought back on the events of our day, or forward to what we might be doing next. I replayed things we had done well and remembered them for the next time, and figured out solutions to problems we encountered in case we found ourselves in a similar predicament again.

There were times when I had no idea where my mind wandered, and simply took in the world around me. Sitting on the back of the bike, with no walls around me, I was part of the landscape. I could look anywhere and find something to engage me. The bike sits me much higher up than a car, so I could glance down into the automobiles as we passed, wondering what stories each person had to tell or where they were going. Sometimes I saw amazing stupidity, like a driver reading a book, steering with his knees while speeding down an interstate, and I'd urge Terry to get as much distance between us as possible. My favorite moments were the sunrises and sunsets, watching the slowly changing colors, and the textures of the clouds as they moved across the sky. I had the time to relax and enjoy it all. Soon I was the one asking for silence, and sometimes the silence would last for hours.

We continued our zigzagging across the south and up the east coast. Stopped for gas in West Virginia, Terry noticed the receipt wasn't good. Going inside the station to get a better one didn't help. We needed to figure out what to do quickly, and we were afraid to ride anywhere and mess up our gas log. Looking around, I saw a bicycle shop next door, ran in and scanned the shop for the smallest, cheapest item I could buy. I came away with a very nice pair of pink cycling socks, and off we went. The East Coast was unfamiliar to us and we were intimidated by the tollways, traffic, and intensity all around us. We dreaded navigating metropolitan areas and feared getting caught in rush-hour nightmares. We were incredibly lucky to time our arrival into New York just before midnight, and although we were pounded by the rough highways, all of which were under some form of construction, we got through the city in good time.

We spent the night in Greenwich, Connecticut, which brought back memories of the two summers I spent there when I was twelve and thirteen, visiting my dad. We headed north through New England, riding by places I had taken my kids on a vacation when they were eleven and nine, and finally made it to Maine, our easternmost state. Starting back west through Vermont and New Hampshire, faced with long stretches devoid of interstates, we meandered on twisty roads behind cars that slowed down on curves but sped up when the road straightened, making it impossible to pass. It was a torturous lesson in patience for Terry.

Terry had changed the configuration on our cell phone, attaching it more securely after our near disaster on the Dam Ride. It was wired into our speaker system and rigged to answer automatically. We primarily used it to call ahead for hotel reservations, but we had given the number to family members in case of an emergency. Riding along in silence somewhere in upstate New York we were startled by a voice saying, "Hey, momma!" We hadn't heard the phone ring and Katie was suddenly speaking to us in stereo, just calling to say hi.

Our route took us through northwestern Ohio, within miles of Terry's family. We had hoped to stop for a quick hello and a meal but realized if we stayed for several hours we could get some needed rest. We'd also be able to coordinate our timing so we could avoid going through Chicago in Friday night rush-hour traffic on the Memorial Day weekend. Our plan worked perfectly, and we again made it out of a major metropolitan area with no delays. One more seedy hotel just north of Chicago, another early morning start, and we were finished with our ride in eastern Montana, eight days and eight hours after starting.

I had visited many places in America over the years, and flown over the country numerous times. Nothing prepared me for seeing it in its totality in such a short time. Rather than seeing the parts, I experienced the whole, and came away with impressions of the unique character of the different regions. The west was endless miles of open space, sagebrush, and grazing lands broken up by intense landscapes, mesas, and canyons carved over eons. Parts of the south were a blur, long stretches of interstates lined with trees blocking the views behind them. There was Utah with its uniform new brick churches and white spire steeples on what seemed like every block, the South with old brick Baptist houses of worship everywhere we looked, and New England and the stone architecture of the Episcopal churches.

We rode through places I had only read about in books or seen on TV growing up, names familiar from the Revolutionary or Civil Wars and the civil rights movement. I was surprised at both the vastness of the country and its smallness. In large cities everything seemed crammed together as people and cars vied for space, with noise and busyness all around. In the rural areas a quiet and peacefulness settled in, and the beauty of farmlands stretched to the horizon. Terry was surprised when the smell of the earth in the cornfields of the deep south brought back such strong memories of his childhood spent on the tractor. The whole was definitely greater than sum of its parts, and experiencing it on the bike, connected so intimately to the environment, was an incredible journey.

Back home we evaluated our ride and saw how much we had improved over the past two years. We had established routines and rhythms. Every detail, from getting on or off the bike, to packing, getting a hotel, and stopping for gas, had a pattern. I used a single word, "Ready," to let Terry know I was settled on the back, my intercom was hooked up, and he could take off. A tap on his shoulder meant I was ready to dismount. Arriving at a hotel, I'd go in and arrange our accommodations, signaling him with a thumbs up if there was a vacancy so he could then park the bike and strip off the electronics. We'd grab our saddlebags and helmets, and with the GPS, radar detector, and cell phone safely removed from the bike and stashed in the backpack, we'd head to our room. We carried packets of hot cereal and titanium spoons and ate breakfast while getting dressed in the morning. Terry went out to the bike, checked tire pressure and oil levels, and re-attached the electronics while I checked us out, and off we went. If possible we stopped at gas stations with fast-food outlets in the same building so I could run in and grab a meal while Terry filled both tanks. Often, fast food meant Lunchables, bite-sized prepacked meals I could tolerate only when riding.

We had routines for paperwork and photographs. Terry logged the odometer readings on each receipt, which I double checked, then he'd put the receipt in a Ziploc bag he kept in a pocket. If we had to take a photo, we'd wait for it to develop, and both of us would check to make sure it had the required elements in it. Then Terry would put the picture into a baggie and I'd clip the camera into the backpack. When we were ready to take off, we'd verbally double check that the receipt had been logged, the baggies stored, the pockets zipped, and the camera stowed, and that everything was attached. We never took off before going through our routine, and we had occasions to be thankful for our habits when we'd realize we would have overlooked something had we not checked. Hearing stories of riders who rode away with all their receipts flying off down the highway kept us from getting lazy. Riding two-up gave us automatic accountability once we got past the idea that it didn't mean the other person was doubting our competence.

On all our rides we tested different combinations and types of socks, shirts, tights, and undergarments to figure out our clothing needs. We pared the clothing down to a minimum using layers and high-tech materials to consolidate what would fit into our limited space. We each wore Under Armour long-sleeve shirts and full-length tights. We preferred having something that covered us completely rather than having our outer gear against our skin. We took a single change of clothes and washed them as needed. My saddlebag had to carry my change of clothes, a pair of lightweight pants or shorts I could put on over my riding tights, shoes to give my feet a break from my leather boots when we weren't riding, toiletries, the hot cereal I ate for breakfast, and my heated Gerbing pants and jacket. Experimenting with different ways to pack, we settled on Eagle Creek compression sacks with labels on the outside of each bag so we could quickly grab what was needed without wasting time digging through the saddlebags. Terry put the bike cover inside my saddlebag compartment, and spare tools and a tire pump on his side.

There wasn't an inch of room that wasn't fully used and there weren't any luxuries along for the ride. After all the rallies we had been in I learned to not care what I looked like, how I smelled, or what other people thought of my hair, which was always flattened from wearing a helmet. I reminded myself I was a fifty-four-year-old woman riding on a motorcycle, traveling all over the country with a man I loved. How many people would even consider doing what I was doing, and whether they approved, I no longer cared. Odds were I'd never see them again anyway.

We averaged 910 miles per day, kept our pace on and off the bike, and maintained meticulous records. We had the confidence we could ride multiple days, through cities and open spaces, day or night, while paying attention to details and working well as a team. We knew this was still only a trial, and that we hadn't needed to take time for route planning or worry about the timing of a bonus. We'd stayed in hotels, sleeping about five hours every night. The only paperwork we really had to deal with was our gas log and keeping track of our state receipts. We hadn't had to stress about photographs being wrong or getting lost, or about missing a checkpoint. But we had ridden hard every day, for ten days straight by the time we got back home. I now had the confidence I had lacked when we were first selected. I now believed we could compete in the Iron Butt Rally.

I had greater respect for all the preparation Terry had done on the bike. He appreciated my route planning, and we had both learned a lot about what equipment was best for our needs and what needed replacing. Instead of being irritated by our different perspectives, we now appreciated them both metaphorically and literally. Terry saw the entire open road ahead of him, while my view included his helmet in front of me. Neither view was correct or incorrect. I saw things he couldn't pay attention to because he had to focus on the road. I was free to let my mind wander, spend time gazing at a beautiful view, or concentrate on reading road signs for him at night so he could watch for animals. I could plan ahead and solve problems before they affected us negatively. He often pointed out things I missed because of my obstructed view. He had to be continually monitoring the road, other traffic, and potential hazards. Together, we were able to experience more than either of us could alone. We valued our unique contributions to the ride, and to our relationship.

We also discussed the irony of experiencing loneliness even though we were riding together. It was such a change from how we interacted at home, where we sit on the couch each night, share our day and talk about whatever is on our minds. We touch frequently and still sit on the same side of the table, enjoying the physical proximity. On our rides, the connection comes from the strategizing and teamwork, not chatting on the sofa. We sit on the same bike, inches apart, yet we never make eye contact. We're covered from head to toe in protective gear, designed to keep us safe from wind, rain, bugs, sun, or any unexpected contact with the road. We talk through an intercom, which makes conversations more stilted. When we stop for gas or a meal, we try to maximize our efficiency, not kick back and relax. Arriving at a hotel, we quickly shower to remove road grime and pass out from exhaustion. Mike Kneebone, president of the Iron Butt Association, once said if you're on a long-distance ride and you aren't riding, eating, or sleeping, you're doing it wrong. What he didn't know is how isolating it can sometimes feel even when you're with someone, so connected yet so apart.

CHAPTER FIFTEEN

Forgiveness

The 2007 Utah 1088, held the weekend of June 23rd, was our final test for the Iron Butt Rally in August. We had worked out most of our kinks in the 48-10 ride, and had a lot of confidence in our routines and teamwork. What could possibly go wrong? Just about everything, as it turned out.

The Iron Butt Rally was now only two months away. We'd overheard comments that we'd only been selected because we were riding as a two-up couple and the IBA wanted more diversification. While I felt insulted and doubted the truth of such sentiments, I also felt we had to ride well and silence the critics. I put enormous pressure on myself to prove we deserved to be in it. I expected us to be brilliant in Utah, planning and riding a winning route without any mistakes. What I forgot is what happens to me when I succumb to pressure, both internal and external. I stop doing the things that have worked well for us and hurry through our routines in a rush to get moving.

Reading comprehension is one of the most important skills in a rally. In a significant change for the 1088, Steve made the first checkpoint at 10 a.m., only two hours after the start. The rally packet included all the bonuses for the entire ride, but the rally itself was divided into three legs. There were only a few bonuses available for the first leg, and they seemed simple. One bonus clearly stated "This is a two part bonus." I carefully read the instructions as "Find these coordinates on your GPS, go there and take a picture," and then "Go to Idaho and buy a lottery ticket." A simple two-part bonus, but impossible to do in the two-hour window. It was obviously a trick, so I dismissed the entire bonus. Terry mistakenly trusted me and did not reread the instruction packet. The remaining bonuses were the slow ride, which we had never attempted, and a low-point bonus right off the freeway near the checkpoint at Cabela's, the sporting goods store that had just been built in Lehi.

We decided to try the slow ride, figuring we had nothing to lose. To calm his nerves, Terry suggested we ride a few miles and then come back to the hotel, knowing most of the other riders would be finished by then and we'd have the course to ourselves. Each rider was allowed two attempts, after which they lost the bonus. Lining up at the tape marker in the parking lot, Terry took a deep breath and gave the Wing just enough gas to stay upright and moving forward. We almost made it to the end mark before Terry had to put his feet down, missing the time by a hair. We made one more pass but missed it by a larger margin. We were glad we had at least tried, although we were disappointed we had come so close and failed.

We stopped in Lehi to take the photo inside Cabela's, and started for the checkpoint. As soon as we pulled back on the freeway, I realized my mistake. I had combined two bonuses into one, thinking the GPS coordinates and photo were a single task. It was now obvious to me that we should have gone to Antelope Island, where the GPS would have taken us, and found whatever was there to photograph. The lottery ticket from Idaho was a completely separate bonus, and, yes, impossible to do in such a short time. Realizing my error, I confessed to Terry, who was then mad at himself for not checking my work. I felt defensive and stupid, and the self recriminations were awful. Instead of coming in with approximately 8000 points, we would have fifty. I couldn't believe I had been so rash in my route planning, and I had a hard time shaking it off. We arrived at the checkpoint and listened to the other riders who had all been to Antelope Island. I was even more embarrassed and humiliated. Terry never blamed me, figuring we both had a part in making the mistake, and tried to boost my spirits. Realizing we had little choice but to sit down with the rally packet, we pulled ourselves together and tried to find a way to recover. This time, we worked closely together, double-checking our work, and came up with a challenging, but definitely doable, plan. I felt better and wanted to get going and get back into the game.

Just before we got to our first bonus on Leg Two, a Mormon historical site, Terry told me we couldn't ride the route we had planned because we wouldn't have enough time. I couldn't believe my ears. Without our aggressive route there was no way we could improve our standings. The rally might as well have ended for me right there. I sat outside the fort and cried in frustration. I felt the last glimmer of hope being snatched away, and I wasn't sure how to get back on the bike and keep riding. Terry sat with me as the very kind Latter Day Saints volunteers, worried I might be sick, came over to make sure I was OK. I finally agreed to just finish the rally and we got on the road again, headed east to our next bonus.

Thirty minutes later, Terry came on the intercom to let me know he had miscalculated his timing. He was now telling me we could have made our original plan work. I couldn't believe what I was hearing. He had forgotten about the one-hour time difference between Utah and Nevada, which would have given us plenty of time to ride to Las Vegas before a midnight deadline. But it was too late to change our plan yet again. I was furious, and couldn't even speak to Terry for quite some time.

"Are you OK?" he asked.

"I will be. Just let me be pissed off for awhile," I answered.

Ten minutes later I came back on the intercom, "OK, I'm done pouting. What do you think we should do?"

"Should we just go back to the hotel? If we're not having fun, then it's not worth it to continue, and right now, I'm not enjoying this."

I could feel myself getting irritated all over again, and had to calm down. "There's no way I'll go back to the hotel. You know how much I hate quitting. Give me some other options."

And with that we debated how to spend the remainder of our time. We surprised Dave McQueeny, one of the rally staff, by showing up early at the second checkpoint, a Subway sandwich store. We pulled out our rally packet as we ate. There were several bonuses available in the eastern part of the state that we wouldn't have had time to get if we had ridden our original plan. The Rally rules allowed us to skip one of the checkpoints, and although we'd lose the points we'd otherwise receive for it, we wouldn't be disqualified. We'd never missed one before, but, as much as we liked Dave, we didn't want to sit and chat with him for two hours until it officially opened. If we used those two hours, we could pick up the new bonuses. We decided we might as well get as many points as we could, riding Leg Three for fun, enjoying the beauty of Utah and being together on the bike. We had nothing left to lose, and it certainly sounded better than returning to the hotel.

By giving up on a decent finish and settling in for a good night's ride, we once again began laughing and having a good time. Instead of being mad, we were joking about how dumb we had both been. It helped that we had both contributed to our mistakes, not because we would have rubbed it in if it had only been one of us, but because we were able to share equally in the self recriminations and in picking each other up. We rode through some parts of Utah I had yet to see, enjoying the solitude of the night and the peaceful early morning hours, all the while surrounded by beautiful scenery. I was reminded over and over why I loved the 1088—it gave us an opportunity to experience such an incredible place, together.

Despite all our mistakes, we still came in about thirty-fourth out of fifty-six, in the low middle of the pack. Because only two couples finished the rally that year, we even came home with a second place plaque. It wasn't the ride either of us had hoped for, but we hadn't completely embarrassed ourselves. Once again, on the long trip home, we spent a considerable amount of time discussing our dismal ride. We were disappointed in our checks and balances regarding route planning, but pleased with how we recovered by focusing on our relationship instead of trying to find blame. I hoped I would learn from this mistake to let go of the expectations of others, and especially those I put on myself.

CHAPTER SIXTEEN

Chesterfield

The Iron Butt Rally would start and finish in Chesterfield, Missouri, just outside St. Louis. In a departure from previous rallies, there would only be two legs, and a single checkpoint, all at the same hotel. Because we have family nearby in Arkansas with whom we'd be visiting after the finish, we decided to drive to the headquarters in our truck camper, towing a trailer with the bike and spare parts. This made it easier to bring our supplies with us, and to pack all we needed into boxes. We planned to have duplicates of everything so we didn't have to do laundry or repack anything in between the two legs, which would free us to focus on scoring and sleeping.

I now had as many lists as Terry. We had clothing lists, snack food lists, toiletry lists, lists of bills to pay, and work and home tasks. I counted out days while making baggies of cereal, medicines, snacks, and anything else that would be depleted over the course of the rally. Terry filled bins with pens, clips, spare batteries, our two Polaroid cameras, and spare film. We put our clothing in compression sacks, and separated all our gear in two boxes, one for each leg. When we arrived at the hotel, we'd bring only what we would need for Leg One into our room, and leave everything else in the trailer to be picked up quickly when we came in for checkpoint. We arranged to have our friend John Parrish fly to Chesterfield to help with changing the wheels and the oil on the bike so we wouldn't waste valuable time going to a dealer. Riding in the truck meant we also had street clothes to wear in the hotel before and after the Rally, a luxury for most two-up couples who have such limited space on the bike.

We filled the camper with food for the trip, planning to sleep in rest areas on our drive and get to Missouri in three days. Jeff Earls, another rider, lives in Portland, and we offered to carry his spare tires and tools to save him the trouble of shipping them east. Our friend Bob Howery acted as our contact person. We'd update him as often as convenient, and he'd pass on any information to others who were following our progress. Two other friends, Jason Goertz and John Downing, both of whom owned Gold Wings, were backups in case we had motorcycle-related questions or emergencies.

One week before departure, while Terry checked the tire pressure on the Wing, the auxiliary fuel cell moved. The spare tank was attached to the back of the bike using a plate with four bolts. The motion of the motorcycle had caused a tear in the plate, and the tank was slowly working its way loose. Terry scrambled to find a welder to help us. He found one only a few miles from us who created a bomb-proof way to attach the cell. We were extremely fortunate to discover this problem before we left. Another couple, Tom and Rosie Sperry, had a similar aux tank that came unbolted during the Rally, shredding their rear tire but fortunately not causing them any harm.

Bike loaded into the trailer, ready to leave for Chesterfield.

As we left Snoqualmie, I felt a mixture of excitement and fear, not really knowing what to expect when we arrived in Missouri. The truck felt slow and heavy compared to riding the bike. We stopped each night in a roadside rest area and settled in for what we knew were our last few good nights of sleep before the big event. We talked over and over about our plans, our strategies, and what we hoped to accomplish. Neither of us had been to an IBR start or finish, and wondered how it compared to the other rallies we had attended. We knew some of the other riders, but there were many we had not yet met.

When we drove into the parking lot of the Doubletree Hotel in Chesterfield Thursday afternoon we were greeted by motorcycles, friends, and strangers. The familiar faces were comforting, and it was nice to see everyone hanging around outside or at the bar chatting and getting to know each other. One of the first riders we met was Chris McGaffin, from Ireland, who had originally planned to ride as pillion with another man, a first for the Rally. Their reasons had to do with costs, splitting everything except the airfare. But the other rider broke his arm just before they were to fly over, and Chris decided to come anyway. He was borrowing a motorcycle from an American rider, and was scrambling to get it rally ready in time for the start.

There were five couples entered in the Iron Butt Rally. Although two-up teams compete head to head with all the other riders, there is a quiet rivalry among them. Looking around, we knew we had some serious competition. The other couples were Tom and Rosie, who had ridden in numerous rallies including the previous IBR; Jim and Donna Phillips, who finished in eleventh place in the 2005 IBR; Reiner and Lisa Kappenberger, who finished second in the five-day Northwest Passage rally; and Bob and Sylvie Torter, whom we knew from the Utah and SPANK rallies. I felt a bit intimidated, but as rookies I also felt the expectations on us were minimal. After the disaster in Utah, I just wanted us to be finishers, to return to Missouri safely, and to have fun riding together. Essentially, I didn't want to do anything embarrassing or stupid.

On Friday Terry unloaded the bike, gave it a once-over to make sure it had survived the journey without any damage, and moved it to the cordoned-off part of the parking lot. People wandered around, checking out the bikes, greeting friends, and sharing stories. We carried our planning supplies up to our room and tried to create some kind of order to help us when we worked on our route Sunday night. We had colored pens, paper maps, our computer, file folders of blank paper, chewing gum, and water bottles sorted in boxes and crammed into different corners of the room along with our riding gear, saddlebags, and street clothes. Keeping the room tidy was a challenge but it also helped keep my anxiety in check. Leg One would be four-and-a-half days, and our plan was to check out of the hotel Monday morning, store everything in the camper, and check back in when we returned. The IBR organizers had worked with the hotel to make the transition smooth so that when we came back we wouldn't have to spend time at the front desk—our keys would be waiting. We'd do this again for Leg Two, so it was critical that we had all our gear organized for easy transport to and from the camper.

Once our room was finished, we went downstairs and joined the others greeting new arrivals. With no other tasks to take care of on Friday, we spent most of our time visiting with friends, sharing meals, and hanging out in the bar. We'd be going alcohol-free starting Saturday, and I'd be going Starbucks-free as of Sunday. After the long drive, it was nice to relax and have a day without pressure. We knew it would all change the next morning when the pre-Rally activities began.

Early Saturday morning we grabbed a quick breakfast and headed outside for tech inspection. A line had already formed and I took my place with the other riders. Knowing we'd be going out on the bike for our odometer check, I came prepared with my protective gear. It was hot and muggy, typical for the Midwest in summer, and I looked splendid in bike shorts, T-shirt and motorcycling boots. I only wanted to put my full gear on when necessary to avoid baking in the heat. Terry waited by the bike for me to get the necessary paperwork, and then went through tech inspection with Steve Hobart, who compared our bike's vehicle identification number to the one on our insurance forms, made sure our fuel cell didn't exceed the maximum capacity, and confirmed that we had all the required equipment in all the right places. This was nothing new for us, and we were quickly finished and ready to go on our odometer check ride.

We lined up on the tape in the parking lot and I read the written directions to Terry—go out to the freeway, ride a few miles, turn around and come back to the exact same line of tape. Our mileage recorded, we headed inside. Unlike other rallies, the IBR took photos of all the riders, made a liability release video, and for the first time, conducted a video interview with each rider or couple. The 2007 Iron Butt Rally was being filmed and made into a DVD about the experiences of the participants, and including an interview with the IBA president, Mike Kneebone, about the history of the organization and the event.

The interview was fun, although I was also a bit self-conscious since I hate the sound of my recorded voice. We were asked why we were riding, what we hoped to accomplish, our riding background, and anything interesting about ourselves. I jokingly threw in the "sit on the curb and talk about our feelings" line. We added in our ages, and our occupations, and the filming was over. Finished with the legal and documentary details, we went to get our shirts and goodie bags, and were essentially free until Sunday afternoon.

Sunday morning felt like a lot of hurry up and do nothing. We were both glad we had taken care of tech inspection Saturday, relieved there were no last minute problems or unexpected hassles. Watching some of the late arrivals, we could see some of the stress of getting everything ready under a time crunch and were happy we could relax. I took a lot of photographs, asked a lot of questions, and tried to remain calm. Terry went over the bike one more time, checking tiny details and reassuring himself that everything was OK. I enjoyed being part of the group, and felt more comfortable recognizing people with whom we'd ridden in rallies or gotten to know since our arrival in Missouri.

In the early afternoon, we had a private, riders-only meeting. As we settled into our seats, I could feel the anxiety building. We really were in the Iron Butt Rally, about to embark on an eleven-day journey we had only imagined over the past year. Lisa Landry, the Rally Master, quickly brought us back to reality with an impassioned speech, reminding us that this was only a game.

Our egos were not dependent on the outcome of this event, and there were people at home who wanted us to return safely. Nothing was worth making her call our next of kin because we'd done something stupid.

She went over some rule changes for 2007. The most notable one for us was that now one of the couple had to be in every photo along with the rally flag. Because one of us had to take the picture of the other one with the flag, we both had to go to every bonus if it involved a tour, hike, or some other excursion away from the bike. Previously only the flag had to be in the picture, which for two-up riders meant someone, usually the driver, could remain resting at the bike while the passenger got the bonus photo.

Next up was Dale Wilson, who told us how the start would take place. He would signal each rider or couple exactly when to leave, and if we angered him in any way, it would not bode well for the rest of the rally. He repeated several times that everyone had to be by their bikes at 8:30 the next morning to have their odometer readings taken, and their emergency cards—which all riders and passengers had to wear around their necks for the next eleven days—hole punched to verify they had them on. Finally, Bob Higdon came up and talked about how to deal with questions from strangers and the press, since the rally is sometimes misrepresented as a race, which it's not. Then Lisa opened the floor to questions, and it was clear there were more than a few anxious riders. We used the time between meetings to go over our preparations one more time, to make sure we hadn't left anything undone, and to give us something to do besides sitting around getting nervous.

The opening banquet for riders, friends, and families started at five, and the excitement in the room was palpable as we went through the buffet line and found our seats. Before Mike and Lisa handed out our rider flags, emergency cards, and rally packs, they made several announcements, including the fact that they had printed the packets on pink paper to make them impossible to fax. This was to prevent anyone from sending a packet to outsiders for routing help. The spirit of the rally was to plan and ride it yourself, without any other assistance. It never occurred to us that people would do that, or that it was something we had to be warned about.

Lisa and Mike also explained the requirements to be a finisher in the Rally. There were four categories—Gold, Silver, Bronze and Finisher—each with higher point values. They encouraged us to aim for a certain number of points in the first leg so we would not enter the second leg with a deficit. If a rider failed to obtain enough points in both legs combined to make it into the finisher's category, they would be scored DNF. Every rider in the room dreaded the thought of that happening to them.

We were finally called up for our number, 23. The twenties were given to those riders who would be going in pairs, either two-up on a single bike, or riding as a two-bike team for the entire rally. There were five couples, and six people riding in pairs—a father and son, a mother and son, and a husband and wife. Once all the numbers were assigned and everyone had their packets, we were allowed to open our envelopes. We were shocked by the number of pages we would have to plow through. There were 123 bonuses for this leg alone. I felt overwhelmed, and while I wanted to run up to our room right away to begin planning, I also dreaded it.

Mike gave an example to demonstrate that it was obvious there were more bonuses than anyone could possibly to go to, and that the challenge was to plan a good route with all the options available. There was a lot of discussion about a bonus at Perce Rock, in Canada. The bonus, which was available only at local low tide, involved crossing the ocean to the rock to take a photo. Tide tables were distributed in the meeting, so it was clear that Perce Rock was a bonus they wanted riders to attempt.

Perce, Quebec, Canada   33,000 points   Available daylight hours

Perce Rock

This bonus requires two photos.

Photo #1: Take a picture of Perce Rock from the bottom of the stairway. Your ID flag does NOT have to be present in this photo. This photo must show that the tide is out! These are fast moving tides; no wading this year Tom! [a reference to an earlier rally when Tom Sperry braved the inrushing tide to get a photo of a lighthouse]

Depending on weather conditions, you may access Perce Rock for approximately 2 hours before and 2 hours after low tide.

Photo #2: Walk out to Perce Rock, place your flag on the rock and take a closer photo.

WARNING: This bonus requires a short walk across the ocean floor; however, the footing is treacherous and should not be attempted unless the water has subsided during a low tide. Tides in this area are extreme and fast-changing, rising 6 to 8 feet per hour!

Perce is located on the eastern end of the Gaspe Peninsula on Provincial Rte-132. To get to the access stairwell, turn right on Rue Biard.

Time: _____ Odometer: _____ Code: REBECCA
Approved: _____

Finally, Bob Higdon gave his traditional benediction—"Do what you can to not embarrass yourself"—and before we knew it, we were heading to our room to tackle Leg One.

CHAPTER SEVENTEEN

The Start

We sat down and took a few deep breaths. Re-reading the instructions helped us focus before we dove into actually planning our route. The Rally staff wanted to make it very clear that it was our responsibility to make sure we not only understood the instructions, but that we had everything we needed before we left Chesterfield.

> Riders, please remember that the Iron Butt is a Rally, not a race. You are put on notice that all bonus locations and in many cases local police departments and/or park police near bonus locations have been notified of our approximate arrival time in their area.

WARNING: DO NOT LEAVE THIS AREA UNTIL YOU HAVE VERIFIED THAT ALL PAPERWORK IS IN YOUR RALLY PACKAGE. THIS IS YOUR RESPONSIBILITY!

Ask Rally Master if there are any changes or corrections.

Before leaving the checkpoint, make sure you can find each bonus location and have a clear understanding of what is required to earn the bonus.

In order to be scored, you must present this bonus listing with score sheet and fuel log. You are free to tear apart and remove any pages that are not needed (for example, on page 10, you decide you will skip all the bonuses in South America, you may remove that page). However, if you lose a page from the bonus listing, you may not claim any bonuses on that page. If you lose the score sheet, it may be replaced at the next checkpoint but it will cause you to receive a 1,000 point penalty. If you lose a fuel log page, there is also a 1,000 point penalty to obtain a replacement

IMPORTANT CAUTION: The following Potential Bonus locations are like a restaurant menu. If you order everything on the menu and eat it, you are going to get sick and perhaps die. Please pick and choose bonus destinations carefully!

NOTE: All times are local!

REMEMBER: *Unless otherwise specified, I.D. Flags are required in all photos.*

When you are out there bonus hunting, *remember,* the bonus is not bagged until you complete the paperwork

We started by entering each waypoint into our computer. I numbered each bonus so we could more easily find them in the rally packet. I read the information aloud while Terry located the address in his Streets and Trips mapping program, and then we assigned a code. Our system included our bonus number, the three-letter code given by the rally, the point value, and any time limitations, either a D for daylight only, a T for timed, or an A for anytime. Daylight meant it had to be completed within one hour of sunrise or sunset. Timed meant the bonus had a specific time frame that must be adhered to.

Going bonus by bonus took a lot of time, and in my usual eagerness I encouraged Terry to move faster. The more I urged him to hurry, the slower it seemed he went. He became irritated with me for pressuring him to speed up, knowing he'd make a mistake. After all our practicing, we still struggled with our different styles under pressure. Once again, our irritation signaled us to stop before we got into an argument. We reminded each other to take a moment to breathe before continuing.

Once all the bonuses were in the computer, we created a map and explored different routes and options. Terry and I know ourselves and our rallying style. We've always shied away from make-or-break bonuses, where if you fail to get the one high-point location the whole leg is lost. Terry was reluctant to try to get to Perce within the narrow four-hour window. The weather forecast called for continued heavy rain throughout the Northeast, and the extra wear and tear on Terry riding in those conditions lessened our desire to head to Canada. Neither of us wanted to repeat the mistake we made in the SPANK rally, where we pushed too hard in the first leg and became exhausted.

There were several high-point bonuses available in the south, which if strung together added up to a sizable number of points, although not as many as Perce. We started to focus on a southern route to see if we could create a reasonable plan. Key West was considered a sucker bonus, attractive but with a high possibility of failure, but given our riding style, it made more sense to us as we looked at our choices. When I saw a bonus in Biloxi, plus several bonuses in and on the way to New Orleans totaling another 16,566 points, I wanted to go. I spent eight days in Louisiana following Hurricane Katrina, providing therapy to first responders in the Department of Probation and Parole. I made such strong connections with the people I worked with I felt compelled to go back. It may not have been the best reason for a routing choice, but it was a very good reason for my heart.

A plan took shape that gave us places where we could add or delete bonuses depending on conditions, which matched our preferred method of riding. It also gave us time to stop each night for just a few hours so Terry could get some sleep. We would head east across Indiana and Ohio, pick up a few bonuses along the way, and arrive at a time-limited bonus in West Virginia before midnight. We'd then head south to Key West, and return to Chesterfield via Louisiana and Tennessee. While Terry converted all the waypoints into longitude and latitude coordinates to be programmed into the GPS, I packed up our nonessentials and laid out our things for the morning. Once we were both finished, we went to bed.

Terry doesn't sleep well before a rally, and it was even worse before the IBR. He kept waking up, re-plotting routes in his head, questioning all of our decisions, panicking that we may have forgotten something. I kept my anxiety and annoyance with him in check. I worried about the toll it would take on him the next day and wanted to tell him to just let it go and get some rest, but I knew it wouldn't help and would only create friction between us. I slept better, but neither of us slept enough.

The Screaming Meanie went off far too early but once we were awake our adrenaline kicked in and we jumped out of bed, showered quickly, and went downstairs to eat our last proper meal for the next eleven days. Terrified of being late, we were by our bike, where we had our odometer recorded and our emergency cards punched, well before 8:30. The parking lot was abuzz with preparations and we joined in the commotion. We mounted the electronics in the proper spots, stowed our saddlebags, double-checked our supply bins in the trunk of the bike, and anxiously awaited the last minute riders' meeting and the start of the rally. The bikes were lined up in two rows facing each other, with ours somewhere in the middle, and behind it all were well wishers waiting to cheer as we took off.

The riders huddled in the aisle between the parked bikes, gathering around Lisa and Dale to hear last-minute instructions.

They explained in no uncertain terms that we had less than ten minutes to get all the bikes out of the parking lot and onto the freeway or the police, who were blocking traffic for us, would be gone. That didn't help calm anyone's nerves. Just then the skies, already dark and foreboding, opened up as torrential rains poured down on all of us and the oil-slicked driveway of the hotel. The rain lessened slightly as we finished up our meeting and headed to our bikes, but my anxiety was now even higher, terrified we'd slip and fall as we made the sharp turn to exit. As we started our engine and watched for Dale's signal, I kept my mouth shut while I silently tried to channel Terry's brain to help him stay relaxed.

Suddenly, the horn on Dale's megaphone went off and he began his ritual of pointing at a bike, then pointing at the driveway, yelling "Go!" and immediately moving to the next bike on the opposite side. One after another we took off. We pulled out, made the turn, and didn't fall. We were officially in the 2007 Iron Butt Rally.

CHAPTER EIGHTEEN

Where's Noah When You Need Him?

The first bonus, inside the Visitor's Center underneath the St. Louis Arch, was practically a given. The three-hour time window and the high point value guaranteed almost every rider would go there, and the assumption was that Dean Tanji or his son Colin would be using the location to catch the action on film. We were not disappointed, riding alongside a car with a camera pointing out the window at the riders as they drove past. While we weren't quite in a line, it was easy to spot all the riders, covered head to toe in protective gear, and their bikes, decked out with auxiliary lights, electronic gear, and auxiliary fuel cells hustling off to the Arch.

Arriving at the designated parking garage, we noticed we'd have to pay when we exited, a bit frustrating for such a short stop but better than having to waste time finding street parking. We quickly dismounted, grabbed the backpack and our camera, and walked as fast as we possibly could in our full gear to the Visitor's Center. As usual, I wanted to hurry and Terry wanted us to slow down, reminding me this was only the first stop and we had eleven days to go. A long line of motorcyclists waited to pass through the metal detector at the front. Jim Owen came up behind us and suggested there might be another entrance further to the south, so we took our chances and followed him. The line was much shorter, but we still had to empty our pockets and backpacks of metal, including keys, chains, and the pocket knives most riders carry for emergencies. Terry hates going through any kind of security, especially if he's being rushed. I, on the other hand, wanted to get on the road as fast as possible. Realizing we were heading for an unnecessary argument, I went in ahead of him and scoped out the mural we needed to photograph for the bonus. It was easy to spot surrounded by all the other riders and flags. Lisa Landry, chuckling at all the activity, was watching from the sidelines.

Terry finally made it through security, and we took our photo and left. The line to enter was even longer now, and it was nice to be on our way to our next bonus instead of cooling our heels with the others. As we hustled back to our bike we saw George Barnes, the winner of the 1999 IBR, running back to the Arch— he had left his helmet inside. It was a good reminder that anyone, even a veteran, can make a simple mistake. Going through our routine, we checked off the list of what was required for the bonus, and made sure we had properly stowed everything before remounting the bike. I had cash ready as we waited patiently in line with the others to pay and leave, all the while being filmed by one of Dean's crew, whom we were sure was laughing at us sitting in traffic. Finally heading east, we were out of St. Louis, across the Mississippi, and on to our next destination. The skies continued to threaten, occasionally peppering us with some drizzle, but we hoped for at least a few hours of good riding weather.

Our luck didn't hold. The deluge came and didn't let up for the next twelve hours. Stopping around noon for gas, we debated waiting for the rain to let up or continuing on slowly but at least making progress. We decided to press on. Terry navigated by following taillights of the cars ahead, keeping a safe distance in case they exited unexpectedly. We were down to forty miles per hour on an interstate designed for seventy. The intense concentration and the poor sleep the previous night took their toll on Terry, who had trouble focusing on the road and had to stop. At a rest area we parked next to a covered picnic table where he could lie on the bench and sleep. We learned on earlier rides that if Terry slept while I stayed awake, he could fall asleep more quickly and deeply because he wasn't worried about the bike. I kept an eye on things, rechecking our plans or calling someone to catch up on news. My fatigue was different from his since I didn't get worn out piloting the bike. I nodded out for perhaps five minutes every now and then while we were riding, letting Terry know I'd be closing my eyes so he would be aware of what was happening.

I called our friend Bob and told him we had made it through the start and were doing OK. He was going to follow the Rally in the daily reports posted online on the Iron Butt site, but we agreed that he wouldn't give us any information about any other riders when I called. After the experience in SPANK with Uncle Bud, we didn't want to know if something bad had happened, nor did I want to know what the other riders were doing so that I wouldn't be tempted to compare our plan to anyone else's.

Talking to Bob helped keep my anxiety in check. I knew Terry needed the rest but I worried the break, along with our slower speeds, would put us too far behind schedule. The major bonus for day one was a timed one in West Virginia, an Iron Butt Association logo painted on the wall at Hoagy's Heroes, a pub inside Hoagy Carmichael's garage. It closed at midnight, and each minute off the bike meant one less minute to make it to the mural.

Getting back on the road, and back into the rain, we headed for Marysville, Ohio, and the Honda motorcycle factory. We arrived during a brief lull in the weather that was causing massive flooding throughout the state, went to the entrance, and asked to go inside the parking lot to take our photo.

Marysville, Ohio   1578 points   Available daylight hours

Honda of America Manufacturing
24000 Honda Parkway

Take a picture of Honda of America Manufacturing

The Honda of America Manufacturing is located approximately 9 miles north west of Marysville, Ohio and approximately 40 miles northwest of Columbus. From US 33 take the Honda Parkway exit north. We will accept any picture of a Honda building at this location (there is both the car and motorcycle factories here, either one is acceptable for this picture).

Time: _____ Odometer: _____ Code: HA
Approved: _____

The officious guard made it very clear we could not take a picture of the buildings from anywhere for any reason, and said he'd call the police if we tried. He offered instead to give us a business card with his name on it. We took a photo of the guard station and driveway after calling Lisa to ask her what to do. Back on the bike we debated if what we had done was sufficient despite having talked with Lisa. We had numerous instances of doubt on the Rally, fearful we'd go to a bonus and get it wrong and lose hard-earned points. But we had to turn our attention back to getting to West Virginia. I was watching the clock, and when Terry told me he needed another break I almost lost it. I was tempted to nudge him along, hoping he could tough it out, but we had learned it was faster to stop and let him sleep. We pulled off into another rest area and he conked out for thirty minutes while I kept my eye on the clock, counting the minutes until I could wake him up.

Getting off the freeway for the final eleven miles to the bonus, our window of time was narrowing quickly. The GPS estimated we'd make it with ten minutes to spare, and our gas gauge was registering empty. We were in small-town rural West Virginia where the stations were few and far between. We were anxious about missing the bonus and agreed to take the chance that the gas station shown on my GPS near Hoagy's would be open twenty-four hours. Pulling up to the side street and the bonus, we jumped off the bike and raced to the back of the house and found the garage with the pub and mural inside. The GPS had predicted correctly—we had ten minutes before we would have missed it. We took the photo of the Iron Butt Association Mile Eater mural, the requirement for the bonus, and slowed down long enough to grab some of the food Hoagy had generously prepared for the riders. One or two stragglers came in after us, and then the bonus closed. There was a gas station a block out of our way, our first real break of the day. All we had to do now was ride back to the freeway, find a hotel where we could dry out, and get some sleep, even if only for five hours.

CHAPTER NINETEEN

Sweat

Waking up to clear skies helped enormously after nearly drowning the previous day, and we were soon riding south through West Virginia to the New River Gorge Bridge. The bonus was a photo of the new bridge taken from the old one, located at the bottom of the deep canyon. The GPS and roadside directions were confusing, and we lost quite a bit of time going the wrong way down a twisty one way road until we finally found it. Sometimes we argued out of frustration when that happened, because each of us felt responsible for figuring out the correct route. I felt pressure to come up with the right answer in seconds because Terry's focus had to be on riding, and I was afraid I'd get it wrong. It wasn't that he'd be mad at me for my directions, but that we'd waste valuable time having to backtrack and correct our mistake.

We arrived just as Rebecca Vaughn, another IBR rider, was putting her camera and flag away. We chatted for a few moments, wished her a safe ride, and watched her take off for her next bonus. We ate a quick snack while enjoying the view of the new bridge which from our vantage point was quite spectacular. We knew we had a long day ahead of us and didn't want to waste any time, but food is essential and it's nice to eat somewhere other than a gas station once in awhile. The road out was much more clearly marked, and we were soon on the highway once again continuing our journey south.

I don't think either of us had clearly thought through the ramifications of riding in full gear, in August, through the southeast. We live in the Pacific Northwest where July and August are our best months, with long, lazy days filled with sunshine and temperatures that might reach 80 degrees. Humidity is a foreign concept for us and summer is the time we plan our best rides, knowing the chance of rain is almost nil. Imagine our surprise when we hit heat, intense heat, and almost unbearable humidity. We had cleverly planned our route to keep us out of the rain, and now here we were with our own personal rain showers inside our Aerostich suits. Full helmets meant we couldn't get relief at stop lights by flipping our face shields up, and I could feel the sweat dripping down my neck. I felt claustrophobic in the heat, and it took a lot of self control to remain calm. The humidity sapped Terry's strength and focus. Gas stops stretched longer as we took an extra few minutes to cool off, removing helmets when normally we would not have taken the time from riding.

We pressed on to the next bonus, a photograph of a giant pink elephant in Hardeeville, South Carolina, then east to Tybee Island and a sculpture of turtles at the base of a water tower. We rode through Savannah, Georgia, and continued out to the island on a small two-lane road, arriving just before sunset. Terry was exhausted from the heat and the riding, and needed to sleep. Lying down on a park bench, he tried to doze off but soon gave up because of the incessant flies. He was in a lousy mood, and angry that we had ridden to Tybee in the first place.

He realized it was a sucker bonus—it had taken far too much time and wasn't worth the 1457 points when balanced against the effort it cost him. His anger wore on me, and I wanted him to just stop talking. We were exhausted and needed to get off the bike. The humidity had worn us out and simply getting out of our gear for a few hours would be a welcome relief. A few miles after getting back to the mainland and onto the interstate we found our next hotel.

When we took off again six hours later, Terry hadn't let go of his irritation regarding Tybee. He kept rethinking what our route could have been if we hadn't diverted so far to the east. I was frustrated that he kept bringing it up and that he had such a hard time letting it drop. It was bad enough we had to deal with the weather—I didn't want to waste energy rehashing our decision. I wanted to get back on the road with a positive attitude and belief in our plan. I held onto the viewpoint that while he was probably correct, what was done was done. In the meantime, we headed farther south into even higher heat and humidity.

Reaching Homestead, we went to the Coral Castle, and once again debated what exactly the bonus required. It said, "Take a picture of the entrance to the Coral Castle," but did that mean the entrance gate, or was there a castle itself inside? Did we have to pay a fee, enter, and get the photo, or was it possible to take only the exterior gate? In a cool hotel room, these directions looked simple, but in a rally, in the heat of the moment, everything seemed to take on much larger proportions and our ability to reason seemed to diminish. Each time we faced these dilemmas we feared we'd mess up the documentation and lose the points. We'd think and rethink what it was we were being asked to do, sometimes arguing with each other about who had the correct interpretation. We finally decided the wording for the bonus didn't require us to go inside when the ticket seller mentioned he'd seen a few other riders come, snap a photo, and leave. We had to stop wasting time and just get going.

We eventually started down the Overseas Highway and the hundred-mile journey to Key West. The traffic was not as heavy as I had feared, although the road was patrolled frequently to enforce the speed limit. The heat was overwhelming me and every time we slowed it was worse. At least when we were moving I got some air flow, but when we were stopped, even for a moment, I started to panic. Luckily, our only stop was a quick one at the Dolphin Research Center on Grassy Key, where we grabbed a photo of a statue of a huge mother dolphin and her calf, and continued south.

There were two bonuses in Key West. One required us to get gas, which we needed anyway, and the other was to take a photo of the buoy marking the southernmost tip of the U.S. We pumped the gas and made our way to the marker for the photo. Terry had doubts about the receipt. He was worried that the thermal paper image was too faint, and that by the time we turned it in for scoring it would be unreadable. We went back for a duplicate. Having come this far, it was worth the extra few minutes to ensure the receipt would be accepted. While the Key West gas bonus was worth only three points, we had to have a good receipt for our fuel log.

Pulling the bike in front of the station's mini mart door, I hopped off to talk with the attendant. A few minutes later a very haggard Terry stumbled into the store, barely coherent. He couldn't follow the simplest instructions and his words weren't making any sense. I realized he was suffering from the heat, and helped him get his helmet and gloves off while urging the clerk to get ice. I pulled his riding suit off his arms and shoulders, and put a baggie of ice on his wrists to cool him off as fast as possible. For several minutes he couldn't focus on anything I was saying, but between the ice and drinking some water, he slowly regained his composure and we figured out what had happened. When we pulled into the station, he thought he had parked the bike under the awning and in the shade, but when we went outside we realized that while the front of the bike was in the shade, the seat wasn't. He'd been waiting for me in the full sun, in his full gear and helmet, in temperatures well over 100 degrees. If he hadn't had enough awareness to come inside, I might have come out to find him slumped over the handlebars.

Driving north from the Keys, Terry was still interjecting little remarks like "If we'd skipped Tybee..." into our conversations and the underlying tension wasn't setting a good tone for the next eight days. This wasn't normal for our relationship. We typically sat down and hammered out what was wrong, and hadn't been able to do that with this issue. I could tell our anxiety was much higher than normal and I was struggling to find the joy and laughter we usually returned to when things were tough. There were some long stretches of uncomfortable silence, and I thought a lot about what was going on.

"Why do you think this is so hard for you?" I finally asked Terry. "You're continually talking about what we should have done and that isn't like you. Even though you aren't accusing me of forcing us to go to Tybee, I feel defensive about our decision to go there. I want to justify it and that isn't helping either of us."

Terry struggled to put his feelings into words. "I keep replaying scenarios in my head, thinking I should have recognized we were behind schedule and pushed harder to skip it. We would have lost those points, but we would have been in a better position to pick up other ones later. I'm mad at myself for not listening to my gut feeling. I knew it was the wrong thing and I didn't trust myself."

"I can understand that. But it's hard on me when you keep bringing it up. It's starting to wear me out, and it's not helping us focus on what's ahead. We need to be okay that we screwed up and let it go. What I don't understand is why neither of us can let it go."

We continued to talk, and it slowly dawned on me that it was the meaning of this rally that was causing our distress. My irritation and defensiveness revolved around my fears of failing so publicly. Every other rally or ride we had been in had been small and private. No one was watching, no lottery was required for entry, and if we failed, we could try again next year. In the IBR, daily reports were posted online, and knowing that they were being eagerly read by thousands of IBA fans magnified my emotions. We had been avid followers of the 2005 Iron Butt Rally and were now part of the group that was being followed. Screwing up would no longer be a quiet affair, it would be published, analyzed, and critiqued. We were competing with some of the very best, and while I told myself it would be honorable enough to simply finish, I didn't want to, in Bob Higdon's words, embarrass myself.

I also now better understood Terry's anger about Tybee. The Iron Butt Rally, known as "The World's Toughest Motorcycling Competition," is to the long distance community what the Olympics are to other sports. Other riders would gladly take our place in a heartbeat. Terry had tried to gain entry once before and failed, and the knowledge that this might be our only chance to ride in it increased his anxiety exponentially. His frustration had more to do with the reality that we had gotten behind our schedule and his fear that we might lose control of our Rally. It was the pressure he put on himself to anticipate problems in time to correct them and the responsibility he felt for the success of our ride that was making it hard for him to let go of Tybee. His optimism that we could push ourselves, combined with his difficulty in changing our original plan when his gut told him he should, created a type of tunnel vision in him. Once he realized his mistake, his tendency was to blame himself.

We shared our thoughts as we continued north. It helped to talk about what was really going on, and Tybee slowly faded into the background. I pulled out my GPS to see what options might be available, and saw that if we stopped for the night near Kissimmee, Florida, we could pick up a daylight-only bonus we would originally have missed due to timing. The tension between us was now history as we checked into the hotel, unpacked our computers, and looked at our original plan. It was obvious that even if we could pull it off, which we seriously doubted we could do, we'd arrive back in Chesterfield exhausted. Making the adjustment to reality instead of what we wished were true, we abandoned our original plan. After our stop in New Orleans, instead of driving northeast through Alabama and Nashville before turning northwest to Chesterfield, we would turn directly north through Memphis, Kentucky, and Illinois.

We went to bed feeling more connected to each other and to what lay ahead than we had the night before. Instead of blaming each other, we'd once again sat on the curb and recalculated. I also better understood my feelings about the Rally itself. No matter how often I verbalized the idea that we were only riding for ourselves, external expectations had a way of creeping in. I couldn't stop those thoughts from intruding, but I could make a choice to bring my attention back to Terry and me, to what we cared about and what our goals were for ourselves.

Waking up before sunrise the next morning, ready to implement our new plan, we drove to the bonus, a landmark fruit stand claiming to be the world's largest orange, the signature export of Florida.

Kissimmee, Florida   2,310points   Available daylight hours

Eli's Orange World

5395 W. Irlo Bronson Memorial Hwy/US 192

Take a photo of your bike in front of Orange World. Make sure some of the 'orange' is visible in your photo.

Kissimmee is located in central Florida, approximately 17 miles southwest of Orlando. Orange World is approximately 2.8 miles east of I4 on US 192/W. Irlo Bronson Memorial Hwy.

Time: _____ Odometer: _____ Code: KF
Approved: _____

What we had forgotten was how frustrating the Polaroid camera could be. It was definitely light, the orange shaped dome was clearly visible with our bike in front of it, and in every photo we took everything looked nearly black. We knew it was faster to wait than to get back on the deserted road looking for someplace nearby open at six in the morning to get a receipt. We kept trying several angles, but ended up having to wait patiently until the sun came up just high enough in the sky so we could get the image we needed.

These tiny annoyances sapped our energy every time they occurred, but we'd force ourselves to quickly regroup and focus on our next destination. This time it was a sink hole near Gainesville, Florida. The bonus stated it was open at 8 a.m. and the photo was to be taken at the bottom of the hole, a hike of some distance down a long stairway. Arriving at the entrance at 8:10, we were surprised to see other riders standing in front of a locked gate, including our Irish friend Chris. Someone was calling Lisa for instructions, but we already understood the rules to be 'take a photo of the locked gate, with the hours if possible, and get an electronic receipt from the immediate area to prove the time you were there.' Not wanting a park ranger to show up and unlock the barricade, I urged Terry to drive down the block to a Starbucks I had noticed in the strip mall we had just passed. I knew the high quality of the receipts and that I'd be able to enjoy my one and only chai tea latte of the rally, drinking it through a straw as we got back on the road. I'm not sure one has tasted as good since.

The Katrina Memorial in Biloxi, Mississippi, was one of the highlights of Leg One for me. I was deeply moved seeing all the debris gathered in the Plexiglas frame, items that washed up in the storm surge during the hurricane. I was anxious to continue on into New Orleans and see the Superdome, where many of the officers I had worked with were stationed during the days after Katrina, and the streets that were piled high with garbage when I was there last. As we rode through the town, I was shocked to see the same markings on the houses, indicators after the flooding of what had been found inside, including living pets and dead bodies, and while the medians of the boulevards had been cleared of trash, so little repair work had been done. People were everywhere, which was a pleasant change from my memories of deserted streets. Bourbon Street, which had been occupied primarily by soldiers and construction workers when I was there, was now opening its doors once again to tourists.

With mixed emotions we took our photos and rode away. I wanted to stop and say hello to the people I had met, whose lives had been so uprooted, and to tell them that they were still in my thoughts and in my heart. But we were on the clock, and the minutes were ticking away, telling us to get going, to head to Memphis. Elvis was waiting.

Memphis, Tennessee   410 points   Available 24 hours

Graceland

3764 Elvis Presley Blvd

Take a photo of the plaque outside the front gate title "Elvis Aaron Presley"

Memphis is located in southwestern TN, near the junction of I-40 and I-55. Graceland is in southern Memphis, from I-55 exit 5 if northbound, exit 5B if southbound.

Time: _____ Odometer: _____ Code: EP
Approved: _____

Finding Graceland was easy, but we were looking for a specific plaque and had no idea where it was. We parked in one of the designated lots the GPS had directed us to, but it was early in the morning and deserted. I walked up and down the street looking for an address or a clue. Another call to Lisa didn't help—she'd never been to this bonus herself. We got back on the bike and rode a bit farther, turned around, and finally found a pedestrian entrance, and lo and behold, the plaque. A lot of frustration for only a few points, but we needed all we could get since changing our route and deleting so many bonuses. The next one, the Tennessee Pyramid in another part of Memphis, was easy to spot alongside the highway and visible from far away. Then we were once again on our way north. A mural in Kentucky, and one last bonus in Illinois, and Leg One would be finished.

We made a quick stop to photograph a motorcycle mural painted on a wall in Paducah, then crossed the Ohio River to Bridgeport—a thrill on the huge span arching over the expanse of water rushing below. The posted speed limit dropped suddenly to 25 miles per hour as we approached the bridge, and we hadn't slowed enough when we hit the slick steel grating. The river seemed to go on forever while Terry focused all of his attention on steering the bike, trying to keep it steady as it wobbled side to side on the uneven, slippery surface.

In Metropolis, the home of Superman, we located the Man of Steel behind the courthouse. We posed for a photo in front of the giant statue, over the words "Truth – Justice - The American Way," using our digital camera so we could keep it as a reminder of some of the unusual places we had visited. It was finally time to head back to Chesterfield, prepare for scoring, have the bike serviced, and get some sleep.

CHAPTER TWENTY

Scoring

At the Doubletree Inn we were greeted by our friend John, who grabbed the keys for the bike and our trailer and went off to gather everything he would need to change our wheels and our oil. In 2007 neither Terry nor I were required to stay with the bike while it was being serviced, and since John and Terry had worked together on the Wing many times we trusted him completely. To avoid the hassle of changing tires, Terry had purchased used wheels and mounted them with new, broken-in tires—all John had to do was swap the entire wheel. Terry made sure he had everything John needed while I ran into the hotel to stop the clock and officially check us in.

Terry and I headed into a small room to prepare our documentation for scoring. There was food for the riders, and we ate while we sorted our paperwork. We made sure all our photos were in the correct order, and picked the photo that best met the bonus requirements if we had more than one. We wrote our name, rider number and odometer reading on each Polaroid, and began going through our gas receipts. To save time while riding, we wrote the odometer reading on each receipt as we got it, then put them in order to fill out the gas log once we were back in Missouri. Early in our rallying days we kept the log while we rode, pulling it out to write in all the details as they occurred, but we learned it was faster and easier to do once we were safely back in the hotel. The log listed every stop we made, with the date, time, city, state, number of gallons pumped, and the price recorded. Any mistake would cost us points. Terry read the information off the receipt, and I wrote it on the paper. We then reversed roles, with Terry reading the information from the log while I double-checked each receipt. Once we began the scoring process, we couldn't change anything, or go back to our room to find a missing receipt or backup photo. It was a laborious process, especially when we were anxious to take a shower and get some sleep.

Photos, receipts and log in hand, we got in line for scoring. We had not, to our knowledge, ever lost points due to careless errors or stupid mistakes, and we did not want the Iron Butt Rally to be a first. Going line by line, receipt by receipt, photo by photo was agonizing, but we appreciated the thoroughness of Don Moses, our scorer. Prior to sitting down at the table, we added up our expected points, and held our breath while Don finalized his tally. We let out a sigh of relief when our scores matched, meaning we had earned every point we had turned in. Leg One was finished. Our total wasn't what we had hoped it would be, but we hadn't embarrassed ourselves. If we kept our points steady on Leg Two, we would at least qualify as Iron Butt Rally finishers.

Checking back into the hotel, we picked up some of our replacement boxes from the camper and took them to our room. Terry looked in on John to make sure the work on the bike was going well. We showered and exchanged gear, packed our saddlebags with clean clothes and more food, refilled our trunk bins with replacement items, and loaded the boxes to take back to the camper. The bonus sheets for Leg Two would be handed out at 4 a.m., and it would be a much more challenging leg. It was finally time for much needed sleep. This leg had only been four-and-half days. The next one was six-and-a-half, but it would most likely be taking us west, into familiar territory.

As I drifted off to sleep, I replayed Leg One in my head. We had worked well creating our plan, taking into account our strengths and our limitations. We'd kept our arguments to a minimum and although we knew when we left the hotel Monday morning that we probably hadn't picked the best route according to the Rally staff, it was one that felt right for us. Battling the rain on day one and the heat the remaining days had taken a toll on both of us, physically and emotionally, but we kept going, taking turns pulling each other out of our doldrums. Our hardest struggle, however, wasn't the weather, but the frustration of letting go of a mistake when we couldn't even agree if we had made one, and if so, how much of one it had been. The "woulda shoulda coulda" game is a brutal one to play, and in my opinion a waste of time unless it was of help immediately. Those reflections were better saved for the armchair quarterbacking sure to come once we returned home. But even with our differences of opinions over where we had gone, we figured out a way to let it go and get back on track. We brought our focus back to us, to having fun, and to working together as a team. Regrouping and deciding to come back to Chesterfield with a bit of extra time to go through scoring enabled us to get some much needed rest, and we were both glad we had decided not to push ourselves to exhaustion on this leg. I was hopeful we would make some better choices on Leg Two, but overall, I was happy we had survived Leg One.

CHAPTER TWENTY-ONE

Heading West

Waking yet again to the banshee wail of the Screaming Meanie, we threw on our clothes and headed downstairs for the distribution of the new rally packets. A crowd was gathered around the position postings for Leg One. We were in 53rd place. The highest standing for a two-up couple was Lisa and Reiner, who were in 33rd. Letting go of our disappointment for only making it into the "Finishers" category in the first leg, we went into the rider's meeting to await instructions and our bonus listing. For Leg Two, there were 134 to choose from, including three in Alaska.

Back in our room, we went through our routine in our slow, methodical way, entering any bonus we thought we might remotely consider, and coding them so we could easily understand our options when we put them in Streets and Trips. We began to study the packet and our map.

Mt Hamilton, California   24,057 points
August 28, 2007   9:00 am to 3 pm
Lick Observatory

This bonus has two parts:

Take a photo of the sign above the archway entrance to the observatory that reads: "Lick Observatory, University of California." Make sure the observatory dome is visible in your photo.

Sign in with Dean Tanji in the Observatory Parking Lot.

Lick Observatory is located on the summit of Mt. Hamilton in the Diablo Range about 12 miles east of San Jose, CA. From I-680 take the exit for Alum Rock Avenue (CA-130), turn east on Alum Rock and ride about 2 miles, then turn east on Mt. Hamilton Road to the observatory There are several telescopes on the mountain. To get to the main observatory you need to make a sharp right turn at the top and follow the road around.

Time: _____ Odometer: _____ Code: LO
Approved: _____

It was clear right away the high-point bonus the Rally Master wanted us to head for was Lick Observatory near San Jose, California. The combination of high point value, the sign-in with Dean, and the limited time window hinted that we again might expect a camera and film crew to be there to take some footage of riders in action. This time, we built our route around the obvious bonus.

There were several major bonuses that were unwise choices for us on the Gold Wing. Mono Hot Springs and the Ancient

Bristlecone Pine Forest were both on extremely difficult roads and Terry didn't have the confidence to attempt either one. Even if we were successful the intensity of the riding would wear him out. We settled on a route west taking I-70, picking up points in Kansas and Colorado, swinging through San Francisco, and ending at Lick Observatory. Our return east would follow I-80 to Salt Lake City, then detour into Dinosaur and Rocky Mountain National Parks before returning to I-70, grabbing the few remaining bonuses in Missouri, and ending up back in Chesterfield. It was a conservative route, giving us an 8000-point cushion to end up as finishers. It had options along the way to add bonuses if the opportunity presented itself. We both agreed on the plan.

We spent about five hours planning and were surprised to see so many bikes still in the parking lot. This leg was complicated, requiring a lot of thought. Unlike the dramatic beginning of Leg One, the start was simple. As soon as we were ready to go we headed to the bike, loaded our gear, and took off. No fanfare, only a few spectators to wish us well, and this time, the weather cooperated. Because the leg started at 4 a.m., we did our planning after several hours of sleep. We hadn't spent the night tossing and turning, questioning all our decisions, and we both felt quite well rested.

Our first stop, the Wizard of Oz Museum, in Wamego, Kansas, was easy to spot. There were other riders coming and going, purchasing any small item to bring back to Lisa, nicknamed the Wicked Witch. In fact, anything with the Witch on it promised "special life credits," although unfortunately, no extra points. I picked out a refrigerator magnet for her and a shot glass for us as a souvenir.

Leaving Wamego, headed for Idaho Springs, Colorado, Terry asked me to recalculate our route and add the Chalk Canyon bonus in Monument Rocks, Kansas. Because the description of the road warned of "several miles of gravel and very fine, loose dirt" it wasn't part of our original plan. It was also a daylight-only bonus and we'd probably arrive past dark, but when my GPS showed it was only a short detour off of I-70 it seemed ridiculous to bypass it without at least checking out the road. I calculated our timing, and unless the gravel was worse than we imagined, it looked like we'd make it before sunset.

The road was hard packed and easy to navigate, and there were other riders ahead of us. Several more were finishing up their photos and getting back on their bikes as we pulled in to take our picture, this time with the sky clearly visible in the background. Returning the same way we came, Terry picked up speed and we were quickly back on the interstate. We stopped early for the night just inside the Colorado border to set ourselves up for a daylight trip into the Rocky Mountains the next morning.

We were on the road by 3 a.m. and arrived in Idaho Springs to take a picture of a giant statue of Steve Canyon, a WWII comic-strip action hero. At a gas station with a McDonalds inside, I bought a bottle of Starbucks Frappuccino from the mini mart and joined Terry for breakfast. Shaking my drink to mix it up, I was immediately covered from head to toe in sugary, milky liquid. In my tired state I didn't realize I had already removed the lid and sprayed it all over myself, the table, and the floor. We looked at each other in astonishment and then began laughing hysterically. Thankfully, the camera was still on the bike. I'm not sure that's a picture I wanted for my souvenir collection.

The intensity of the cold surprised us as we rode into the mountains. We'd been in crippling heat and humidity only days before and now we were wearing our heated gear to keep from freezing as we rode up the switchbacks to the 12,095-foot pass. In our Utah rallies, we'd ridden in blistering 109-degree heat in the afternoon and freezing 30-degree cold only eight hours later. Over the past few years we'd ridden in torrential rain, incredible winds, blowing snow, unbearable heat, and intense humidity, unable to comfort ourselves with either a heater or air conditioner. Being on the bike forced us to constantly deal with the elements.

The road was beautiful, and at one point Terry spotted a mountain goat on a hillside. I was captivated by the scenery, looking out over meadows and streams in the crisp morning air. The sky was perfectly clear and blue. We arrived at the designated sign for Independence Pass, took our Polaroid shot, and spent a few minutes shivering while enjoying the spectacular views. A group of mountain bikers unloading their van offered to take our picture with our digital camera, giving us another memento of our trip. Succumbing to the cold and the demands of the clock, we hopped on the bike and rode back down the difficult, twisty road. Terry started showing some of his characteristic signs of exhaustion, shaking his head and responding more hesitantly to my questions. It was a challenge for him to make it to the gas station we had passed in Leadville where he could stop to take a much needed nap. I went into the mini mart, bought a newspaper, and spent a few minutes reacquainting myself with what had been happening in the rest of the world while we were so intensely focused on the Rally. I truly had no concept of current events—I'd lost all sense of time other than when we had to be at our next bonus.

Our third stop of the morning was Tennessee Pass and unlike the road to Independence it was an easy ascent and a quick return to I-70. With no more bonuses on the day's schedule, we rode west toward California and Tioga Pass into Yosemite Valley. In my younger years I camped and backpacked in the valley, and knew the area well. I also knew what it could be like in the middle of summer, filled with recreational vehicles, tour buses, and crowds. I wanted us to be on Tioga Road no later than 6 a.m., ahead of all the slow traffic that clogged the two-lane highway as it climbed over the Sierras. Using my GPS to calculate time and distance, I suggested we ride another few hundred miles and stop in Ely, Nevada, earlier than usual, and sleep for five hours. That would give us a solid 950-mile day, and we could be back on the road by 1 a.m. to ride the 350 miles to Tioga and on into Yosemite.

Before leaving the hotel in the middle of the night we made a call to an answering machine monitored by Tom Austin. There were three call-in bonuses during the Rally, with two on this leg. They were easy points to get by phoning within the specific time window. Tom had drilled the required information into us— location, location, location—and we wrote our notes on a piece of paper before calling to make sure we didn't mess up.

Call-In Bonus - no specific location   2,077 points
Available August 27, 2007

Call 916-XXX-XXXX and leave the following information:

Your name, your rider number, your location (city/town and state/province), the last bonus you scored, and the next bonus you are headed for. While it is not required for this bonus, if you have a quick story, please leave it also!

Time: _____ Odometer: _____ Code: CI Approved: _____

I'm still shocked by how quickly we made it in and out of Yosemite. Coming through Tuolumne Meadows and crossing the valley before climbing again to Glacier Point, Terry kept his attention on the narrow, twisting road. I tried to describe the beauty all around us, saddened that he had never been here and would have so few images by which to remember it. Leaving the bike in a small parking lot, we hiked together to the overlook at Glacier Point and took our photo with Half Dome in the background. We paused for just a moment so he could enjoy the view before getting back on the Wing and heading back down into the valley where the road was already clogged with tour buses heading up. I shuddered at the thought of being stuck behind all that traffic with no room to pass and time ticking away.

A quick stop for a picture of a plaque outside the door of the Ahwahnee Hotel and we had successfully navigated Yosemite. Stopping for gas on the way out of the park, we ran into Greg Marbach, our friend from SPANK and now a fellow IBR rallyist, heading into the valley. Unlike the Utah 1088, where most of the riders are somewhere within a single state, on the IBR, with all the bonus choices available and the size of the country, it's weird to run into other riders in such random places. This time, however, I wasn't worried how his, or anyone's, route compared to ours. I was just happy we were finishing Yosemite while he was just starting.

Half Dome from Glacier Point, Yosemite.

Thinking we wouldn't be out of the park until later in the day, our original plan was to ride to San Jose and get the required rest bonus, putting us in a good position for the ride up Mount Hamilton to Lick Observatory the next morning. But now we were far ahead of schedule. It was only 10 a.m. and Livermore was a short 150 miles away. We took off down the mountain with fingers crossed that we'd find an open fire station. The instructions for the fire station were as follows:

"Take a picture of the Centennial Light, the oldest continually burning bulb in the world, on since 1901. You will need to go into the Fire Station and ask to see the light. Go to the door and ring the bell. You MUST also sign the guest book as we will be monitoring it! If the fire personnel are out on a call, you must wait for their return."

We arrived to find an empty station. Not sure what to do or how long to wait, Terry took a short nap. I studied our maps to see if there were other bonuses we could add if we stayed ahead of the clock. I called Bob to chat and help keep me alert. Thirty minutes passed. I was pacing the parking lot, unsure what to do, when a fire truck pulled into the driveway. I shook Terry out of his slumber and ran over to the crew to say hello.

Terry asleep in the Iron Butt Motel.

"Bet you've had quite a few people stopping by today," I said.

The firefighter looked at me oddly as he climbed down from the truck. "Um, I'm not sure what you're talking about. This isn't our station. We're just here for a minute dropping off some supplies and taking off again."

"Would it be OK if you let us in to get a picture of the light bulb?" I asked as they were unloading boxes.

"What light bulb?"

My heart stopped. How could it be a famous landmark and a local crew not know about it? What if they couldn't find it? What if it required a special key?

"Oh, is this it?" he called as the bay doors opened, revealing a tiny wire attached to the ceiling with a small bulb dangling at the end.

I breathed a sigh of relief. Had I been sleeping along with Terry the truck would have come and gone, no one the wiser. We took our photo, with Terry lying on the floor to get me, the flag, and the light in the picture. We signed the guest book, thanked the crew for letting us in, and waved goodbye as we rode off.

CHAPTER TWENTY-TWO

All Systems Go

Our original route took us into San Francisco the day after we went to Lick Observatory. But it was now early afternoon on the day before, and we had plenty of time to go to the city and pick up the six available bonuses. I'm familiar with San Francisco and I had no fears about riding the narrow, busy streets or going up and down the steep hills. I wasn't sure, however, about the optimum order for getting to all the locations. I was trying to figure it out on the GPS when I discovered a button for "Auto route" and tapped it. Viola! It quickly plotted the shortest path to get all the bonuses, and I directed Terry to each one.

We stopped at the bottom of Lombard Street to take a picture of part of "The World's Crookedest Street" with the motorcycle in it. Terry pulled over next to a parked car, I jumped off, took the shot with him sitting on the bike, and before other drivers got upset, we were off. We had similar luck with the other three bonuses before crossing the Golden Gate Bridge to take a picture of the Wing with the orange span visible in the background. It took a few shots before we were able to get the photo without the fog blurring the image.

Before we knew it we were back in the city standing in a dirt parking lot overlooking the Sutro Baths, once a large, privately owned swimming-pool complex built in the late 19th century, now abandoned after the building housing the baths burned down in 1966. The instructions said we could take a photo from where we were if the ruins were in the shot, but if not we had to walk down the steps until they were "clearly" visible. We wasted time debating which part of the baths were "the ruins" because neither of us wanted to hike down the steep wooden steps in our boots and gear. We finally agreed we had taken the correct shot and, with no further bonuses on our list, discussed what to do next.

Terry suggested adding the Boardwalk in Santa Cruz, only seventy-six miles away. It was already five in the afternoon and I doubted we could get there in time given the heavy rush-hour traffic on both I-280 and Highway 17. I was in my cautious mode and unsure whether it would impact us later on. Terry convinced me we should at least try. We needed to ride south anyway to spend the night and get our rest bonus, so we could decide whether it made sense to go over the mountains to the coast when we got into San Jose.

As we rode, Terry reasoned that we didn't have much to lose since our next bonus, Lick Observatory, wasn't available until 9 a.m. the next day. If we stopped now, he said, we'd spend the evening sitting around wasting valuable time, and I agreed with his logic. I figured we could always stop if things weren't going well, and when I added up the hours I had to admit we didn't need that much sleep. When I-280 started to back up we took advantage of lane-sharing, one of the benefits of riding a motorcycle in California, which helped with our timing. Even when the cars stopped we kept moving, and soon we were at the exit for

Highway 17. It was clearly worth the attempt to go to Santa Cruz, and surprisingly, the traffic thinned and we made excellent time over the mountain pass.

I had visited Santa Cruz with my kids a few years earlier and spent time at the Boardwalk, the oceanside amusement park where we had to take a picture of the Welcome sign, so it was easy to find the bonus. Pulling the bike up in front of the entrance, I hopped off and took the photo with Terry holding the flag. A few minutes later, while we gassed up the bike and had a quick snack, Terry insisted yet again on checking for bonuses we might find before giving up for the night. I was a bit more resistant at this point and felt we had accomplished enough for one day. But he was adamant that we at least look, and when we found one, Bixby Bridge, a daylight-only bonus sixty miles away just south of Carmel on Highway 1, and programmed it into the GPS, it looked like we might just make it. I had no logical argument against trying, so we got back on the road and raced off towards Big Sur.

My heart was pounding and my adrenaline was flowing as we rode down the twisty highway watching the sun dipping below the horizon. I now wanted this bonus as much as Terry. We had exactly one hour past sunset to get the picture, and the minutes were ticking away. The photo had to include the arched super-structure of the span as well as the historical bridge sign. The sky was still bright as we pulled into the turnout for the bridge and snapped the shot. Black. Another shot. Again, black. We took a photo of the horizon. Black. The limitations of Polaroid film were ruining the bonus for us. We took photo after photo, close-ups of the bridge, the sign, Terry holding the flag covering the reflective tape on his Aerostich, until we had several photos that clearly documented we had been in the area, although none that showed the bridge itself despite it being clearly visible in the evening light.

To get credit for the bonus we now needed to prove we were in the area during the specified time window. We were on a remote stretch of Highway 1 with nothing in sight and we needed a computer-generated receipt. We couldn't believe we'd come this close and lose it because of a stupid piece of paper. I suddenly remembered seeing a sign for Rocky Point, a restaurant about three miles back up the road. Praying it was open, we raced back up the highway and turned down the narrow driveway where I hopped off the bike, ripped off my helmet, and ran inside.

"I need a receipt, for anything, and I need it fast!" I pleaded with the startled maître d' as I ran in the door. "I'll pay for anyone's drink, appetizer, whatever, I just need a receipt!"

He wasn't sure what to do, but finally led me into the bar where I ordered a Sprite and paid the $2.50 with my credit card, just to ensure the proper paperwork. Leaving a five-dollar tip, I thanked them profusely and ran back outside.

"I got it!" I yelled to Terry, waving the receipt in my hand. The time stamp was 20:37—less than ten minutes to spare. We high-fived and celebrated our success, then carefully documented the odometer reading and put everything away securely. This was one receipt I did not want to lose.

Rest Bonus – no specific location   7,723 points   Must start on Tuesday, August 28, 2007

Stop for 5 or more hours. Document this stop as follows:

___ at the start of the rest period, obtain a dated, time receipt from a location, for example, a gas station, a motel, a store, etc.

___ at the end of the rest period, obtain a dated, time receipt from the same location

Our preference is that you also include your motel receipt with this bonus if you motel it, however, it is not required.

WARNING: We are giving you wide latitude on this bonus with few restrictions so that you may have the flexibility to use it as needed. However, we want to stress that if you are caught bending the rules in the slightest, you will be expelled from the rally. This bonus DOES NOT mean "get a receipt and go collect bonuses", it means stop and rest.

Time: _____ Odometer: _____ Code: R5
Approved: _____

Riding back to San Jose at a more leisurely pace, I used the GPS to find a hotel near the turnoff we'd be taking in the morning for Lick Observatory. We called on the bike phone and made a reservation so we could finally relax the last few miles. We talked about our day and how, because of our decision to stop in Ely so early the night before, we had been able to pile on so many bonuses and were now in the enviable position of being ahead of our plan as we headed back east. Unlike we'd done on Leg One, we were using our strategy to add, instead of delete, bonuses. I had to admit Terry's pushing us had been exciting, and certainly paid off. We'd ridden a nine-hundred-mile day, through one of the country's busiest national parks and one of its busiest cities, and trusted each other's decisions. Luck had played a part, but we had taken advantage of every opportunity thrown our way.

CHAPTER TWENTY-THREE

Adding Up

The morning came quickly after a much needed night's rest. We planned to get to Lick an hour before the bonus opened to allow for any complications along the way. We no longer needed to go into San Francisco, and had the advantage of turning east when we came off the mountain. We hadn't decided what we would do other than ride into Sacramento to take a photo of a giant Coca-Cola cup and add two bonuses in Grass Valley. Terry insisted on going to Guru Lane in Gerlach, a 200-mile detour on a two-lane road only a few days before Burning Man. I figured we'd take each bonus one at a time as they got closer.

We started toward Mount Hamilton through fields and valleys, a short seventeen-mile trip from our hotel. The last seven miles wound up a steep, narrow road that took every ounce of Terry's skill to navigate. Coming around one sharp, upward angled hairpin turn, Terry suddenly stopped. Letting the bike slowly roll backwards a few feet, he once again accelerated, executing a three-point turn to prevent the bike from falling over. He had to repeat this maneuver a few more times before we reached the top. He was exhausted and a bit shaken when we pulled into the observatory parking lot. We were greeted by several other early arrivals and spent some time relaxing and watching Dean set up the canopy where we'd all have to sign the official attendance roster. Terry sat by the bike and as he tried to unwind from the tension of the ride I reassured him he had done a great job on such a challenging road.

I sat in the shade and talked with another rider who had just realized he wasn't going to have enough points to be a finisher. No matter how hard he tried to reconfigure his route, he came up short. He told me this was his last chance to be in an IBR and he was devastated. I felt so badly for him, knowing he couldn't recover from earlier mistakes and decisions, and now he had to decide if he wanted to complete the ride and return to Chesterfield or just go home.

Some of the riders were taking their bonus pictures. I asked Dean if the official time, 9 a.m. to 3 p.m., meant the photo had to be taken within that window. "The bonus is open from nine to three," he said. I took that as a yes, so we waited while I read and reread the instructions. This was the major point bonus of this leg, and I didn't want to show up at scoring and find out we'd blown it.

At 9 a.m., as I stood in the growing line of riders waiting to sign in, Dean officially opened the bonus. He stamped my rally book and Terry and I went over to take the picture, making sure to include the name of the observatory as well as a portion of its dome, the two requirements. Double-checking all our work, we were ready to pack up and take off. Dean asked us which way we were heading out, and I mistakenly told him the wrong way. We later found out he wanted to tape us leaving as part of the *Hard Miles* DVD, and the road we were taking wasn't the one he wanted. I think about that every time I watch the movie and see the rider they filmed, knowing it could have been us.

Elated that we had our big-point bonus out of the way, we took a different, much less technical road out of the mountains and quickly found ourselves on I-580 heading toward I-5 and north to Sacramento. Terry noticed another rider coming up behind us and wondered aloud why he seemed to be driving erratically. I turned to look as he came up on our right side. He seemed fine, even waving as he passed us. Terry double-checked his mirrors and realized the right one was dangling precipitously. The driver hadn't been erratic, our mirror had been.

Getting off at the next exit, we found a dirt lot and pulled over to assess the damages. The bolts holding the mirror assembly on had worked loose and only one remained—barely. Had Terry not noticed the other bike behind us, he might not have discovered the problem until it fell off. Unable to come up with a solution to re-attach the mirror securely enough that we could continue riding, we turned to our old standby, duct tape. Rather than being upset, we started laughing at our situation, giddy after our long morning.

Once again, duct tape to the rescue.

With our patched bike looking like it had a wounded right wing, we got back on the interstate and found our way to Sacramento where we easily spotted the giant Coca-Cola cup and took our photo. We had both agreed to add Grass Valley and the two bonuses there to our list, and followed the GPS as it took us on thirty-six miles of twisty backroads to the old covered bridge. We then rode up and down the street trying to find the Kneebone Cemetery. It was off the road a short distance across a dirt parking area and through a broken-down chain-link fence. We wandered through the family graveyard until we found a suitable headstone with the Kneebone name engraved on it. Terry held the flag while I took the photo.

We stopped for a few minutes to eat a snack at an old picnic table nearby. We were startled to see Brian Roberts, another Rally rider, walking up. He had similar trouble locating the cemetery and was happy to have found it as well. He confirmed that the road we'd be taking out was much shorter and easier than the one we'd come in on. He told us that he'd taken his rest bonus the night before at his home in Nevada. It's not recommended for a rider to sleep at home during a rally because the temptation to linger is so high. But Brian is such an experienced rider that it posed no problem for him. After we said goodbye to Brian, Terry and I had to settle the question of whether to go to Gerlach.

Terry's reasoning was simple. The bonus was over 6000 points, it was a familiar road, and we'd be riding right past the turnoff on I-80. He was becoming more aggressive about getting points following our successful ride the day before. By adding in the unexpected bonuses, we had increased our potential finisher's status by 10,000 points, and he was hungry for more. My argument was that the road would be long, hot, and jammed with cars. He was more insistent than I had ever seen him, and I knew if I didn't go along with him, he'd be really disappointed. He wanted us to push ourselves and not get complacent. Once again, he won, but I don't think I really fought him that hard.

We were both right. The road was packed with every kind of vehicle imaginable, filled to the brim with furniture and people. Burning Man is a counterculture festival in the middle of the Black Rock Desert of Nevada, a dry lake bed about a hundred miles northeast of Reno. It's reached by a two-lane road that's usually empty, but once a year 80,000 or more party goers descend on the area to build a city, complete with streets and yards filled with couches, beds and art. At the heart is a giant sculpture of the Burning Man, looming over the landscape. At the end of the three-day festival, he's set on fire, and the next day the town disappears.

We were stuck in the parade of craziness. City, county, state, and tribal police patrolled the road, keeping everyone in check and enforcing the speed limit. The hundred-mile ride, which can usually be done at a brisk clip, was torturously slow. I felt an "I told you so" coming on but kept my mouth shut. I had agreed to go, and we were already committed, so my commentary would do nothing to improve the situation. I chuckled at the oddities poking out of the open pickup trucks, and had flashbacks to my childhood as the *Beverly Hillbillies* theme song played in my head.

Surprisingly, as we neared the main street in the tiny town of Gerlach, the traffic lightened and we rode the final mile out to Guru Lane in relative peace. Pulling off the highway and parking in the small dirt clearing, we hiked the path to the IBA memorial site. It was Terry's first visit, and neither of us felt a need to rush. We took our time, paying our respects before heading the hundred miles back to the interstate.

The ride back to I-80 was much faster since all the traffic was headed the opposite direction. The three extra bonuses had added more than 12,000 points to our total, and I was beginning to believe we might actually have a good chance at improving our standings. I wanted to calculate our score to see how we might do, but Terry wisely suggested not tallying our points anymore. We already knew if we were able to get to the remaining bonuses in our original plan we'd be finishers, and he didn't think the extra pressure would help our decision making. He wanted us to decide bonus by bonus if it made sense to add one based on timing and energy. My competitive nature wanted to see the numbers piling up, but reluctantly I agreed.

The next leg of our ride was 500 miles without a bonus in sight. After the intensity and excitement of the past two days it was hard to slow down. Our normal pattern was to stop each night for almost five hours sleep, and Terry proposed we grab two hours in a rest area and continue to push ourselves a bit harder. No longer a princess who needed a bed and four walls, I had spent many a night on a picnic table and had no problem sleeping in my full gear and helmet. The anonymity gave me a confidence that no one would bother me since they had no idea if I was a male or female stretched out next to Terry. We stopped somewhere near Elko, Nevada, a mere 750- mile day, but one without Terry taking a nap. Before nodding off, we set our Screaming Meanie, made our next call-in bonus, and then slept soundly. Back on the road while it was still dark, we took our photo of Wendover Will, a giant neon cowboy greeting gamblers as they came into West Wendover, and continued on to Salt Lake City.

CHAPTER TWENTY-FOUR

Dinosaurs and Lightning, Oh My

The sun came up as we arrived in Salt Lake City just ahead of the morning commute. We easily found the full-size painted buffaloes on the front lawn of the Council Hall Building and continued east for several miles on I-80. Turning off the interstate, we rode through the Wasatch Mountains on Highway 40, a familiar road from our 1088 rallies. Somewhere near Vernal, Terry said he needed a nap, and while he slept I sat on a bench surrounded by a quiet valley and called our friend Bob with an update. This time I wasn't upset with Terry because I knew our short stop the night before would mean he'd be tired sometime during the day.

The challenge on a rally is not lingering in any one place too long, and dealing with the frustration of seeing things you want to visit but can't. We'd always wanted to spend time in Dinosaur, hiking and learning about the area. This wasn't going to be our chance. We took a photo of the stegosaurus sculpture outside the visitor's center and got on the road toward the next stop, Milner Pass, a daylight-only bonus 250 miles away. The GPS predicted we'd be cutting it short.

The sun had already set when we arrived at the sign for the Continental Divide. In the parking lot we saw two bikes, and from their equipment it was obvious they were in the Rally. As we walked out to the overlook, we were greeted by Alan Barbic and Tom Melchild, who were riding as a team and were taking a moment to enjoy the view. We took our photo of the sign with our flags, and then turned to take one of the sky with the trees in the foreground. This time the Polaroid captured the image with sufficient light and we knew we had our proof—there was no need to rush off to find a receipt. Grand Lake was twenty miles behind us down the twisty road we had just climbed, and Estes Park was thirty miles ahead, too far to reach before the time window closed.

The route to Estes Park took us over the Rockies on the Trail Ridge Road. We had never been in the area and had no idea what to expect. The cliff-hugging highway—the highest paved through road in the country—reaches an elevation of 12,183 feet, with sharp drop-offs along its narrow path. As we climbed, Terry kept his full attention on the road while I described the spectacular views he was missing. Even in the failing light they were incredible. He kept mumbling about the conditions, hoping it stayed paved the whole way. The "Road Work Ahead" sign indicated otherwise, and we were soon riding on dirt and gravel for short stretches behind cars, trailers, and tourists.

The sky was threatening, a light drizzle was already falling, and we both crossed our fingers that we could make it over the pass before the weather cut loose. At the top the road leveled off briefly. All at once there was a terrifying flash of light, a tremendous boom of thunder, and the radar detector shrieked at full volume with a piercing tone we'd never heard before.

"Holy shit! What the hell was that?" I screamed.

"Lightning! Let's hope there isn't any more!" Terry yelled, his voice shaking. "I just want to get off this damn road before it gets any worse!"

We had no idea where it had struck, but it was far too close for comfort. It took us a while to calm down, and even longer for the ringing in our ears to stop. The dark had now fully enveloped us, and as we rounded a sharp turn before beginning our descent snow began falling. We turned another corner and came to a STOP sign and a one-lane road. As we chatted with the flagger, the crews worked furiously into the night. Wiping snow off our visors, we started laughing, wondering if a swarm of locusts or some other pestilence was soon to follow. Luckily, the micro storm quickly passed, the flagger let us go, and as we headed downhill we finally relaxed.

Sixty miles later we reached I-25 near Fort Collins. Terry was exhausted. He wanted to stop for another two-hour break and we began to argue. I thought we needed a good night's rest in a bed and if we stopped for less than that we'd be wasting time. He had become aggressive in the last two days and thought we could just keep pushing on with the same intensity. We had learned on earlier rides that sometimes it's better to give in and sleep than try to limp along with short breaks. This time I was insistent, and he conceded. We checked into a hotel and spent a few minutes figuring out what to do the next day before passing out. We were still well ahead of schedule, and Terry suggested riding north to Nebraska to pick up three bonuses totaling almost 10,000 points. I was in full agreement with his plan.

Waking up four hours later we were greeted with dense ground fog outside. It was so thick it was impossible to see even the taillights of trucks, forcing us to creep along for the next fifty miles until the sun finally made an appearance. Our first stop was Scottsbluff National Monument, a daylight-only bonus. It was only a 150-mile ride, but it felt like it took forever with the fog. The instructions said we had to ride approximately 1.25 miles into the park and take a photo of a marble bench. We rode up to find a locked gate and the Visitor's Center closed, so we took a picture of the barricade and headed into the nearby town of Gering and a McDonald's for breakfast and a receipt. Bumping into yet another rider, Mike Langford, we joined him for a quick bite and some small talk.

Our next bonus, Chimney Rock, was a roadside photo of a plaque with the unique landmark in the distance. Continuing on to Alliance, we saw Carhenge, a replica of Stonehenge assembled on the plains of Nebraska. The sculpture is made of vintage American automobiles with their noses planted in the ground and covered with gray spray paint. We met Art Gavin there, finishing up his photo before taking off. He offered to take a picture of Terry and me with our digital camera, one of our favorites to this day. We played leapfrog with Art for several hundred miles before heading off in different directions somewhere west of Omaha.

Terry and I had some heated conversations during our ride on the interstate. I was pleased with all the risks we had taken and was beginning to get paranoid about something happening in the final hours of the rally, blowing our chance to be finishers. I had no rational basis for my fears—the bike was running fine and Terry was feeling strong—but I kept having images of road construction or bike failures only miles from the hotel. We had seen it happen to our friend Jim Owen on the last day of the 2005 Rally. But Terry had no intention of getting back to the hotel eight hours or more before the penalty window opened and regretting not pushing harder. He didn't want a repeat of the SPANK Rally, where our timidity in Leg Two had cost us a strong finish.

I dug in my heels and so did Terry. We pulled off the highway and sat on the curb. I wanted confirmation we could go after the extra bonuses in Iowa and still have a two-hour cushion for our arrival in Chesterfield. I also wanted to build in two hours for Terry to sleep, knowing he'd need it at some point. He pulled out the GPS and showed me we could add the miles and still address my concerns. I still wasn't convinced. He continued pleading his case, and I could tell he cared deeply about our decision. Reluctantly, I conceded. I had no idea what it would mean in the point count or our final standings, but I did recognize it would make a huge difference in Terry's feelings about our rally.

"You have many cars in this photo."

We would need to maintain close to a BBG pace on the final day of an eleven-day event. This meant an average speed, including stops, of about 62 miles per hour for the next twenty-four hours. We had never ridden with such intensity and with so much at stake. There was no time to goof off—we had to rely on our preparations and routines to make sure we didn't make a stupid mistake this late in the game. Once we decided to add Iowa, I had to be completely on board and fully support everything we did. The chances of error only went up as the pressure and exhaustion built.

CHAPTER TWENTY-FIVE

The Final Push

Following I-80 we took the exit for Elk Horn, Iowa, and found not only the Danish windmill bonus but another of the couples in the rally, Bob and Sylvie. There was no time for chat, just a quick wave hello as they rode off and we took our photo. A bit farther down the interstate we took the exit for Patriot Rock, a twelve-foot-high granite boulder once known as "Graffiti Rock" by the locals. High-school kids used to cover it with slogans, mascots, and love notes. Several years ago nineteen-year-old Ray "Bubba" Sorenson II saw the movie *Saving Private Ryan* and was inspired to paint the rock as a tribute to veterans. He paints a new mural on it every year.

Terry had served in the Navy and we had close friends who were in Iraq. This was not a bonus we wanted to rush past. We stopped for a moment and paid tribute to the service men and women we knew, and to all who had lost their lives protecting our country. Brushing away our tears, we wished we could have spent more time admiring the painting, but had to be content to add it to our list of places we might return to someday.

King City, Missouri, was 120 miles away and the clock was ticking. It was getting dark and we had to keep moving. Our next bonus was an old gas station built in the shape of a huge, red electric gas pump with two regular-size pumps out front. On one of the rural backroads we were passed again by Bob and Sylvie, who we figured were already ahead of us. I had a moment's hesitation when I thought we might have bypassed a bonus we hadn't noticed, but when I pulled out my GPS I confirmed we were on the right route. We guessed they had stopped for gas and were now catching up. As we pulled up the street trying to find the pump in the now pitch-black sky they passed us yet again going the other direction, having just finished taking their photo.

Another challenging Polaroid moment. The pump is huge but it's situated in the middle of a large field with no lighting. Pulling the bike onto the grass and using the headlights to illuminate the scene, we were joined by another Rally rider who saw what we were doing and brought his bike alongside ours. Between us we were able to focus just enough light to get our pictures. This was really getting old.

We needed gas and pulled into a station not far from the Big Pump bonus. We kept bumping into others as we got closer to the finish, and this time it was Tobie and Lisa Stevens, one of the couples riding the Rally together but on separate bikes. We needed a break, so we chatted for a few minutes and grabbed a snack. I knew Terry would get tired at some point and need to sleep, but food would sustain him a while longer. We wanted to keep going as far as we could before taking a longer stop.

Chatting with other riders and grabbing a snack.
(Photo courtesy of Tobie Stevens)

I was increasingly anxious about our time and how far we still had to go. We had to make Chesterfield before 8 a.m., after which time penalties started accruing. We'd lose a hundred points for every minute past 8 we were late until 10 a.m. when the window closed and the Rally ended. Anyone who arrived even a second late would be disqualified. The GPS indicated the mileage alone would take us a minimum of six hours and it was already past eleven. We had nine hours, including sleep and gas breaks, to finish.

Terry hit the wall just north of Kansas City and couldn't go any farther. We'd ridden almost 850 miles since we left Fort Collins that morning, but we were still almost 350 miles from Chesterfield. He had to get off the road, and so did I. Neither of us wanted to risk pushing any farther without a serious nap. We found a rest area along the interstate and pulled into a dark corner where we could park the bike close to a picnic table. Covering the front of the bike to hide our electronics and stuffing the

backpack with our camera and rally pack between the handlebars, we set our duplicate Screaming Meanies for two hours and
put the alarms on their highest setting. Terry lay down on the
bench while I climbed onto the top of the table and settled in
to sleep.

I couldn't nod off. I kept having images of someone sneak-
ing over to the bike and stealing our backpack. I wasn't worried
they'd take the GPS, the phone or the iPod, only the backpack,
and with it the rally packet and all our dreams of being finishers.
I climbed off the table and grabbed the pack. Lying back down,
I threaded my arms through the straps, fearing someone would
steal it if it were sitting on the table. I held the Screaming Meanie
firmly in my hand, afraid someone would take that, too. Clearly,
I wasn't quite in my right mind. I kept thinking about our IBA
number, and how desperate I was to earn one in the low hundreds. We were so close and I was frightened something would
snatch it away.

CHAPTER TWENTY-SIX

The Clock is Ticking

I found everything intact when the Meanie woke us. The rest area was still dark, the bike was where we left it, and the backpack was in my arms. Shaking off the vestiges of sleep, we rode through the parking lot past two other riders sprawled on tables and grabbing some shuteye before the final push home.

A photo of the sign at the headquarters of Garmin, the maker of most of the GPS units used by long-distance riders, in Olathe, Kansas, was our second-to-last bonus. We expected to see other riders as we all began migrating back to the barn, and we weren't disappointed as we rode up to find Andy Mills on his Victory Vision. Andy was testing the bike's performance under the harsh conditions of the Rally. He told us the bike was handling beautifully and he was having a blast. Making quick work of the photo, we put the flag and camera away, logged our mileage, and headed back to I-70. It was now 1:30 in the morning and we still had 250 miles to the finish line with one more stop to make.

We needed to fuel the bike one last time and stopped somewhere east of Kansas City. We took a short break and removed our helmets so we could eat a quick snack. Terry pumped the gas, filling the main tank and the auxiliary cell that held enough gas to make it back to Chesterfield.

The fleece neck gaiter I was wearing for warmth had gotten twisted inside my jacket and was bothering me.

"Can you tuck this back in for me?" I asked Terry. "I can't reach the back to do it myself."

"I can't," Terry said. "My hands are dirty." He held them out for me to see.

I stared at him incredulously. "Seriously? Do you really think I care?"

Neither of us had showered since the hotel in San Jose, three days ago. Our stop in Fort Collins had only been for sleep, and we had spent two nights on picnic benches in our gear and our helmets. Dirt was the least of my worries. We laughed at the absurdity of what he had just said and what we were doing—standing at a gas pump in the middle of the night, filthy, stinky, and having the time of our lives.

Our last bonus, on the campus of the University of Missouri, was situated on a large lawn with no place close by for the bike. We weren't sure where to park and the only lot we found was marked "Faculty Only, Permit Required." In our tired state we actually struggled with whether it was worth the risk to leave the bike there. We decided the campus police would probably not be too worried about a motorcycle stopped for ten minutes at 3:45 in the morning, and the odds of a stranger stealing our GPS were equally remote.

Columbia, Missouri   1,910 points   Available 24 hours

University of Missouri

Take a photo of the six Ionic columns that are a symbol of the University of Missouri.

Located in central Missouri near the junction of I-70 and US-63, from I-70, take exit 126/Providence and go south to E. Broadway and turn east to S. 9th Street. Turn right and park near 9th and University Avenue. From that corner, walk west onto campus and the columns will be directly in front of you.

Time: _____ Odometer: _____ Code: CM
Approved: _____

This was our final battle with the Polaroid camera and with the correct interpretation of instructions. Did it literally mean all six had to be in the shot? Impatiently waiting the thirty to sixty seconds for each exposure to develop, we'd check only to find we had could barely see five of the six. Eight pictures later we agreed we had one where we could just make out the shadows of the last column and called it good. It was clear we had been there and we would take our chances at the scoring table. We needed to get moving.

The last hundred miles are a blur. My brain kept running through worse-case scenarios of massive traffic jams, two-hour construction delays, or the Wing breaking down on the side of the road. I feared Terry would get too tired and need more sleep, and that if he did I'd want to strangle him. I could taste victory and was paranoid it would be snatched away. Finally turning onto I-64 and the last stretch of highway, I felt the emotions starting to bubble up inside. Terry, on the other hand, was struggling. He had no problem keeping the bike going, but wasn't sure what to do as I pointed out road signs. Instead of saying "Take exit 19," I gave him turn-by-turn instructions.

"Get into the right lane, get off the freeway *now*. Turn left *here*, stay in this lane, turn left *now*. Turn right into this driveway *right here*. Turn left at the end of the hotel *here*."

We pulled up to a cheering crowd. The sky was still dark, with a thin band of light starting to form on the horizon. I was overwhelmed by emotion. I couldn't stop the tears from falling as Terry tried to maneuver the bike into a parking spot.

"We did it! We did it!" I kept shouting, waiting for him to join me in celebrating our finish.

"Why are all these people in my way?" he mumbled. "They need to get out of my way, I need to park the bike."

For a few moments he had no idea of the magnitude of what we had done, or even where we were. I tried to get his attention and hug him as I sat for a moment on the bike. He just wanted me to get off and let him put the sidestand down. I jumped off the bike and tried once again to hug him as he dismounted, but he couldn't take it all in. I needed someone to share my joy. Turning, I saw George Zelenz, our SPANK Rally Master, and hugged him instead. Terry focused long enough to put his arm around me as someone took our picture, and we ran into the hotel to stop the clock. It was 6:15 a.m.

"We did it! We did it!"

CHAPTER TWENTY-SEVEN

The Finish

Unlike after Leg One, we didn't have to rush through scoring in order to get some sleep. We had plenty of time for that over the next several days. Instead we splashed water on our faces and got something from the breakfast buffet provided for the riders. Pulling out our rally packet, photos, and receipts we began getting everything in order. This time I was grateful for Terry's compulsiveness in making sure we had everything. We double- and tripled-checked our work. We didn't want to take any chances of being dinged for an accounting or paperwork error. Terry wrote down each bonus on a separate sheet and tallied them up, including the points for the two call-in bonuses and our emergency cards. We were shocked. If we didn't lose any points we had pulled off an incredible Leg Two.

We stood in the hallway waiting to be called in for scoring and chatting with other riders. The energy was contagious despite everyone's exhaustion. We spoke with someone who was obsessing about his picture of the Sutro Baths and whether the ruins in his shot were correct. He was convinced his photo would be rejected, and as we talked to him my own anxiety skyrocketed. This was the same question we'd had when we were there, and his interpretation was making me nervous. Did we get it wrong? If we had, Terry reminded me, there was nothing we could do about it now.

Don Arthur, our scorer, was a friendly, no-nonsense Navy man. He greeted us warmly, commended us on arriving safely, and invited us to sit down and begin the process. His demeanor turned serious as he methodically went through our gas log and photos. We sat quietly, letting him do his work and only answering questions if he raised one. I held my breath as he looked at our picture of the Sutro ruins, but he simply glanced at it, said, "Yup," and gave us the points. Pulling up our photo of Carhenge, he paused.

"I'm sorry, I can't accept this bonus, it's not the correct photo."

I couldn't believe my ears. Tears sprang to my eyes. I panicked and started to say something, to plead our case. Terry reached out to grab the rally packet to reread the directions.

Don sat and stared at us. "The instructions state take the picture with *one* car in it. You have *many* cars in yours." My heart sank. How could we have known the bonus was that specific? We hadn't understood the packet to mean *only* one car.

"Just kidding," Don deadpanned after an interminable pause. Chuckling, he wrote the 4327 points on our score sheet. We didn't know whether to hug him or kill him.

We didn't lose a single point in either leg. The feeling was incredible as Don stood and shook our hands, congratulating us on an excellent ride. I wanted to jump up and down, yell and scream and cry all at the same time. I couldn't wipe the grin off my face and neither could Terry. We had finished the Iron Butt

Rally. All that was left was the finishers' banquet where we would hear the final standings and learn our new IBA numbers. Before we could enjoy our evening, however, we needed a shower and sleep.

Rested and refreshed, we joined our fellow finishers downstairs for dinner, drinks, and celebrations. I bounced from table to table taking pictures, hearing stories, and sharing our excitement. I also saw riders who hadn't made it because they hadn't earned sufficient points or had had bike problems. Chris, our Irish friend, who was on his first visit to the U.S., hadn't fully understood the sheer size of the country and the time it took to ride from place to place. He had come up 13,216 points shy of the 190,000 needed to be a finisher. He vowed to return and try again.

Another friend, Ken Morton, had taken his photo of Lick Observatory very carefully after the 9 a.m. opening time, but forgot to get a portion of the dome in his picture. That cost him 24,057 points and a Silver Medal finish—another reminder how easy it was to make a simple yet costly mistake. Alex Schmitt broke a wheel 140 miles from the hotel. Although he found a local rider who loaned him a sportbike so he could make it in on time, the penalty for changing bikes—50 percent of his points—cost him a potential podium finish.

Ninety-seven motorcycles had started, and by the end only sixty-four qualified as finishers. There had been one accident and many bike failures. Terry's decision to stop adding up our points as we rode had been the correct one. We chose our bonuses based on time, not pressure, rode a great ride, and finished safely.

Starting with the last-place finisher, the names of the riders were called one by one. Each walked to the dais amid applause to receive their plaque and a handshake from Mike Kneebone and Lisa Landry. As their scores were announced, we held our breath, not knowing where we stood in comparison with the others. Three of the other couples were called up and we were still sitting.

"In twenty-ninth place, riding two-up on a Gold Wing, Terry and Lynda Lahman."

We were stunned. We never expected to recover from the first leg as well as we had, to move from 53rd to 29th. After our mediocre first leg, we had shaken off our disappointment, regrouped and ridden a solid Gold-level second leg. Not only had we finished the Iron Butt Rally, we had done it in a way we could be proud of. We'd set out with three goals, and we'd met them all. I knew, standing next to Terry, the man who had been "out there somewhere," that I'd already won gold. We had fun riding together, working as a team, taking risks and pushing ourselves. We finished, joining the ranks of select group of people who have completed "The World's Toughest Motorcycle Competition." The Silver Medal plaque Mike handed us was our final hard-earned bonus.

Epilogue

We covered 9,397 miles in eleven days and rode harder than we had ever done before to achieve our goals. If we had stayed with our original route in the second leg we would have finished in 58th place. Adding the twelve bonuses and pushing ourselves boosted our standings by almost thirty positions. We kept our focus on what was important–our relationship–in the midst of exhaustion, confusion, and doubt. In three short years we moved from dating to finishing the Iron Butt Rally. We shared an intense experience that most people outside the long-distance riding community will never understand, and earned a place in a brotherhood known to only a few. What makes it even more special is we did it together, on the same bike.

Terry told me early on in our relationship that he was always practicing his riding skills. He'd go out in all kinds of weather, anticipating problems so he would have an idea of what to do should one occur suddenly and demand an instant response. He never believed passing his driver's test was the end of his learning. Riding year round kept his knowledge fresh, and it was part of what made riding with him feel safe for me.

This became the blueprint for our marriage. We spent our time continuously practicing, building the skills we would need to be successful, making room for our strengths, our weaknesses, and our differing perspectives. We found ways for both of our voices to be heard, taking the time to sit on the curb when sometimes we'd rather have just kept on riding, avoiding the hard work that made the marriage seem so easy.

Riding two-up, navigating the small space we had to share, learning what was essential for us, came to define our marriage.

We each came into the relationship with baggage, and together we figured out what was necessary to carry with us and what was weighing us down or simply taking up space. Out of those decisions came an intimacy we both had been seeking. Neither of us wanted to be on separate bikes, riding in parallel but not feeling connected. We had experienced that in our previous marriages. We wanted to share the pain and the joy of having to give something up to gain something more.

When I chose to ride on the back of the bike with Terry, I was making a choice to trust him with my life. Falling in love meant trusting him with my heart. Learning to let the bike guide me and to suspend my need for control allowed me to let go of taking responsibility for every move we made. But I knew I would not be content as simply a passive partner, whether on the bike or in the marriage. Making the decision to ride long distances and to compete in rallies challenged me to find a way to contribute. Having to navigate the fine lines between controlling and trusting, speaking up and letting go, helped me find a way to share in the responsibility of our relationship. As we became equal partners on the bike, each finding our place, we were also becoming equal partners at home.

When I was contemplating my post-divorce world I imagined I'd be content living alone, connected to my family and friends and enjoying a variety of activities. Growing up, I thought my grandparent's marriage was a fantasy, a romance novel about finding the perfect person and living happily ever after, something I had no interest in pursuing. After meeting Terry, I realized that romance is not simply in finding the person who "gets you," but is created in all the choices made after that moment.

The choices we made were to be open and honest, to push our limits and admit our failures, to share in the victories and to hold onto each other when faced with defeats. We simply chose to do it together, on a motorcycle, a thousand miles at a time.

Notes and Credits

Special thanks to Steve Chalmers/MERA and Mike Kneebone/ Iron Butt Association for information and permission to reproduce bonus listings and other materials used in this book.

Hard Miles, the DVD made during the 2007 Iron Butt Rally, can be purchased through the Abracadabra Presentation Graphics, Inc. website: http://abracadabra.pro/corporate-video/ hardmilesdvd.htm.

More information about long-distance riding and the Iron Butt Association can be found online at http://www.ironbutt.com.

Iron Butt Magazine can be purchased through the IBA website: http://www.ironbutt.com/ibmagazine.

Steven M. Hobart granted permission for the cover art. Additional examples of his photography can be found on his website, Overland Motorsports Photography: http://www.olmsp.com.